# Cottage Witchery

*A Book of Shadows & Practical Magick*

## Kimberly Renee

Copyright © 2024 Kimberly Renee

All rights reserved

The characters and events portrayed in this book are fictitious. Any similarity to real persons, living or dead, is coincidental and not intended by the author.

No part of this book may be reproduced, or stored in a retrieval system, or transmitted in any form or by any means, electronic, mechanical, photocopying, recording, or otherwise, without express written permission of the publisher.

ISBN-13: 9798346486596

Cover design by: Kimberly Renee

Printed in the United States of America

# Disclaimer

The content presented in "Cottage Witchery: Book of Shadows & Practical Magick" by Kimberly Renee is intended for informational and entertainment purposes only. The author and publisher do not guarantee the completeness, reliability, or suitability of the information contained within this book. Readers are encouraged to approach the practices discussed with discernment and personal responsibility.

Cottage witchery and related practices are deeply personal, and results may vary based on individual beliefs, experiences, and circumstances. The author does not claim to provide expert advice on health, spirituality, or any other subject matter. Readers are advised to seek professional guidance where necessary.

By engaging with the material in this book, readers acknowledge and accept that they are participating at their own risk. The author and publisher shall not be held liable for any direct or indirect damages, losses, or adverse effects resulting from the application or interpretation of the information provided herein.

Cottage witchery is a path of exploration and personal discovery. It is important to respect the diverse beliefs and practices within the wider spiritual community. Always exercise caution, critical thinking, and an open heart as you embark on your own journey.

## Other Books by Author

Angel Magick: Empowering Your Magickal Practice with Celestial Energies

Baking Magick: Whipping Up Magick in Your Kitchen

Bewitching Cocktails: 100+ Recipes of Enchanted Cocktails, Potions, Spells & Rituals

Coastal Magick: Discovering Magick by The Sea

Cottage Witch's Crystal Magick

Cottage Witchery: A Beginner's Guide

Cottage Witch's Apothecary: A Practical Guide to Herbalism, Oils, Spells & Rituals

Cottage Witch's Kitchen Witchery: Stirring Up Magick in The Kitchen

Cottage Witch's Faerie Magick: Potions, Spells & Rituals

Cottage Witch's: Guide to Potion Oils: Recipes, Spells, and Rituals

Cottage Witch's: Guide To Self-Care Recipes, Spells & Rituals

Cottage Witch's: Teas Brews & Potions

Moon Magick: Unlocking the Mysteries of Lunar Energy

Out of The Broom Closet: Embracing Your Inner Witch with Pride and Power

Simply Natural Witchcraft: Grimoire for Everyday Magic

Smudging: Guide to Creating Sacred Spaces

The Bewitching Baking Grimoire: A Spellbook of Charms, Recipes, Rituals and Spells

The Priestess Mysteries: Ancient Wisdom for The Modern Sacred Woman

White Witch: A Comprehensive Guide to Positive Magick

White Witchcraft: A Beginner's Guide to The Craft

Witchery: Revealing The Magic Within

Yuletide Baking

Yule: Celebrating, Decorating, Spells & Rituals for the Modern Witch

# Cottage Witchery

## Book of Shadows & Practical Magick

# Preface

As I pen these words, I find myself nestled in the cozy embrace of my home, surrounded by the fragrant herbs and vibrant blooms that have long inspired my journey into the world of cottage witchery. It is within these humble walls that I have cultivated not just a garden, but a sacred space where nature's wisdom intertwines with the threads of my own lived experiences. This book, "Cottage Witchery: Book of Shadows of Practical Magick," is an invitation to join me on this enchanting path, where the ordinary meets the extraordinary, and where every day holds the potential for magic.

Throughout my life, I have found that true magic is not solely confined to the grand gestures or dramatic rituals often depicted in stories and films. Instead, I have discovered that it flourishes in the quiet moments—in the flicker of candlelight as I sip herbal tea, in the whisper of the wind through the trees, and in the laughter shared with loved ones around a simmering pot of stew. This book is a collection of those moments, a tapestry woven with practical spells, meaningful rituals, and heartfelt reflections that celebrate the beauty of a life infused with intention and gratitude.

Cottage witchery is not just a practice; it is a way of living that honors the rhythms of nature and the wisdom of our ancestors. It invites us to reconnect with our roots, to release the weight of modern distractions, and to embrace the simplicity and abundance that surrounds us. Each page of this book is a step towards embracing your own unique path, encouraging you to listen to your intuition and to find joy in the everyday magic that unfolds around you.

As you journey through these pages, may you discover the power of your own creativity and connection to the world. Let your heart guide you, and remember that, like the seasons, magic is ever-evolving. I hope this book becomes a cherished companion as you delve into the traditions of cottage witchery and craft your own Book of Shadows—a personal testament to your explorations, discoveries, and the love you weave into the fabric of your life.

With warmest wishes for your journey ahead,

*Kimberly Renee*

# Contents

Title Page
Copyright
Disclaimer
Other Books by Author
Cottage Witchery
Preface

| | |
|---|---|
| Chapter 1: Introduction to Cottage Witchery | 1 |
| Chapter 2: Creating Sacred Space | 8 |
| Chapter 3: The Book of Shadows | 16 |
| Chapter 4: The Elements of Nature | 23 |
| Chapter 5: Plant Magic & Herbalism | 30 |
| Herbal Teas | 40 |
| Herbal Oils | 41 |
| Herbal Salves | 42 |
| Chapter 6: Seasonal Celebrations & Sabbats | 44 |
| Chapter 7: Kitchen Witchery | 51 |
| Chapter 8: Moon Magic | 58 |
| Chapter 9: Crystals & Gemstones | 65 |
| Chapter 10: Divination Practices | 77 |
| Chapter 11: Spirits of the Land | 85 |

| | |
|---|---|
| Chapter 12: Candle Magic & Spellcrafting | 91 |
| Chapter 13: Intention & Visualization | 97 |
| Chapter 14: Community & Collaboration | 102 |
| Chapter 15: Animal Guides & Familiar Spirits | 107 |
| Chapter 16: Crafting Magical Tools | 112 |
| Chapter 17: Deities & Archetypes | 124 |
| Chapter 18: Shadow Work | 129 |
| Chapter 19: Grounding & Protection Techniques | 134 |
| Chapter 20: Remedies & Recipes | 140 |
| 1. Herbal Infusions & Teas | 141 |
| 2. Healing Salves | 143 |
| 3. Essential Oil Blends | 146 |
| 4. Bath Soaks & Scrubs | 148 |
| 5. Tinctures & Extracts | 150 |
| 6. Magical Infusions | 152 |
| 7. Crafting Homemade Candles | 154 |
| 8. Homemade Laundry Solutions | 160 |
| 9. Homemade Beauty Products | 164 |
| 10. Homemade Perfumes | 169 |
| Chapter 21: Sabbat Recipes | 173 |
| Samhain (October 31 - November 1) | 174 |
| Yule (Winter Solstice - December 21) | 179 |
| Imbolc (February 1 - 2) | 184 |
| Ostara (Spring Equinox - March 21) | 190 |
| Beltane (May 1) | 196 |
| Litha (Summer Solstice - June 21) | 201 |
| Lammas (August 1) | 206 |
| Mabon (Autumn Equinox - September 21) | 212 |

| | |
|---|---|
| Chapter 22: Magical Correspondences | 218 |
| Chapter 23: Your Path Forward | 227 |
| Glossary | 231 |
| Resources | 235 |
| Bibliography | 237 |
| Personal Thank You | 241 |
| About The Author | 243 |

# Chapter 1: Introduction to Cottage Witchery

∞∞∞

As the last remnants of daylight slipped behind the horizon, casting a warm golden hue across the trees in my backyard, I took a moment to pause and breathe. It was the kind of evening that wrapped around you like a familiar blanket, bringing with it a sense of comfort. But beneath that comfort lay a curiosity that had been bubbling within me for months, ignited by whispers of a world I had yet to truly explore—the enchanting realm of cottage witchery.

My journey began quite unexpectedly. I had always admired the beauty of nature: the delicate dance of leaves in the wind, the intricate patterns of frost on windows, and the soft glow of candlelight during long winter evenings. Yet, it wasn't until I stumbled upon an old, dusty book at a local thrift shop that the spark of cottage witchery was truly ignited. The book, titled "The Herbal Lore of Wise Women and Wortcunners: The Healing Power of Medicinal Plants," seemed to call out to me from the shelf, its spine slightly cracked, and its pages tinged with the scent of forgotten herbs.

As I flipped through the pages, each word felt like a secret revelation. I learned about the magic of herbs and how they could be used not just for cooking but for healing, protection, and even divination. There were recipes for potions, love and wellness, and rituals. Before I knew it, I was fully immersed in a world where nature and intention intertwined.

That weekend, I started small. Armed with a few herbs from my kitchen—basil, rosemary, and thyme—I decided to create a simple herbal sachet, meant to promote calmness and clarity. I tied the herbs together with a piece of twine, focusing my thoughts on tranquility and peace as I worked. As I held the sachet in my hands, I felt a rush of energy; it was as though I was connecting to something much greater than myself.

But it wasn't just the herbs that fascinated me. I began to learn about the significance of the moon phases and how they could influence the energy of my spells and rituals. It was a chilly evening when I stepped outside with my first intention for the new moon—a heartfelt wish to embrace this new journey fully. I lit a small candle, watching the flame dance in the gentle wind, and whispered my intentions into the darkening sky.

The more I delved into cottage witchery, the more I found that it thrived on simplicity and presence. My tiny home transformed into an altar of sorts; I carefully curated a space filled with plants, crystals, and handcrafted candles. I made it a point to take weekly walks in the nearby woods, collecting fallen leaves and wildflowers, allowing nature to guide me in my practice. In those sacred moments, I felt an undeniable connection to the earth, and I felt supported by its wisdom.

Over time, I found solace and empowerment in this practice. I discovered that cottage witchery was not solely about performing rituals, but about cultivating an awareness of the small magic around me—the way sunlight filtered through the leaves, the comforting scent of fresh herbs, and even the warmth of my cup of tea as I took time for myself. Each small act felt like a stitch in the tapestry of my life, binding me closer to the magical essence that existed in the ordinary.

The more I learned, the more I wanted to share this newfound passion. I began hosting cozy evenings at my home, inviting friends to craft their own herbal sachets and learn about the magic of nature. These gatherings became a beautiful blend of laughter, stories, and shared intentions, weaving together a community centered around empowerment and connection.

As autumn descended and life became more hectic, I found refuge in the rituals I had established. A simple cup of herbal tea, a nourishing meal cooked with intention, and a moment of meditation under the stars became my sanctuary. In embracing the magical world of cottage witchery, I discovered not just a practice, but a way of living—one that grounded me in the present and connected me to the whispers of the earth.

And so, on quiet evenings when the world seemed to pause, I would often find myself sitting on my porch, a candle glowing softly beside me, the scent of fresh herbs wafting through the air, and a heart full of gratitude for the magic that exists all around us, waiting to be discovered. It was in these moments I truly understood that we all have the power to cultivate our own magic, and for me, it had started with the gentle, wise embrace of cottage witchery.

## Introduction to Cottage Witchery

Cottage witchery, a gentle and introspective practice within the broader realm of witchcraft, is a celebration of simplicity, homeliness, and an intimate connection to nature. I would like to introduce you to the fundamental tenets of cottage witchcraft, the sacredness of home and hearth, and personal reflections on the transformative journey of becoming a cottage witch.

## Definition and Principles of Cottage Witchcraft

Cottage witchcraft can be defined as a practice that emphasizes the use of natural materials, household items, and everyday rituals to create magic within the context of one's home life.

Rooted in a rich tapestry of folklore and tradition, cottage witchcraft does not require elaborate altars or extensive rituals; instead, it highlights the beauty and magic of the mundane.

The principles of cottage witchcraft focus on:

1. **Connection to Nature**: Practitioners often emphasize the importance of seasonal changes, local flora and fauna, and natural cycles. This approach encourages a deep appreciation for the world around us and suggests that we are inherently woven into the fabric of nature.
2. **Simplicity**: At the heart of cottage witchery lies the idea that magic can be found in the simplest of actions and materials. From stirring a pot of herbal tea to setting out a few stones collected from a walk in the woods, cottage witches learn to see the magic inherent in the ordinary.
3. **Home and Hearth**: The home is viewed as a sacred space, a vessel for magic and healing. Rituals often incorporate domestic tasks—cooking, cleaning, and crafting—turning everyday activities into sources of enchantment and intention.
4. **Self-Sufficiency and Sustainability**: Cottage witchcraft often promotes sustainability through practices such as gardening, foraging, and cooking from scratch. This self-sufficient lifestyle fosters a deeper awareness of the resources we consume and the gifts that nature offers.
5. **Community and Sharing**: Traditionally, cottage witchcraft is about creating community. Cottage witches often share their knowledge with family and friends, cultivating bonds through the act of creating and sharing magic, food, and wisdom.

Through these principles, cottage witchery offers a pathway for individuals to reclaim their personal power and foster connection with the world around them.

## The Significance of Home and Hearth in Witchcraft

Home is much more than a physical shelter; it is a sanctuary for the spirit. In cottage witchcraft, the concept of home extends beyond walls and furnishings to encompass the emotional and spiritual landscapes they hold. The hearth, traditionally the heart of the home, is where families gather, meals are shared, and warmth is provided.

## The Hearth as Sacred Space

The hearth has historically been a site of worship, symbolizing not only physical warmth, but also emotional security and divine presence. In cottage witchery, the hearth represents the home's heart, a place where intentions are set, and gratitude is expressed. Many practitioners create a small altar or designated space in their kitchens or living rooms, where they can honor the elements, seasons, and spirits of their ancestors.

## Rituals of Daily Life

Incorporating witchcraft into daily life transforms mundane activities into sacred rituals. Cooking is perhaps one of the most accessible forms of magic in cottage witchcraft. With each stir of a pot or sprinkle of herbs, practitioners can infuse their food with intention—be it love, healing, or protection. Cleaning, too, is a form of magic: as one clears away clutter, they create space for new energy and blessings to flow.

## Creating a Sacred Atmosphere

The ambiance of one's home plays a crucial role in fostering a magical environment. From the scents of freshly baked bread to the glow of candlelight during evening rituals, cottage witches cultivate a space that reflects their intentions and desires. This environment becomes a canvas for their practices, encouraging mindfulness and presence in each moment.

**Personal Reflections on Becoming a Cottage Witch**

The journey to becoming a cottage witch is uniquely personal, often rooted in childhood memories of family traditions and the natural world. My path began as a little girl enchanted by the stories of wise women in my grandmother's tales, who conjured potions and danced in the moonlight. Those whispers of magic ignited a spark within me, a yearning to connect with the earth and my home.

As I matured, life's responsibilities threatened to extinguish that spark. A busy career and the hustle of modern living clouded my ability to see the magic around me. However, a pivotal moment arrived during a long, solitary winter. Stripped of distractions, I found myself drawn back to the kitchen, where I began to experiment with herbs, baking bread, and creating simple floral arrangements. It was there, amidst the flour and fresh herbs, that I rediscovered the joys of cottage witchery.

Through this practice, I learned to embrace both the chaos and the calm of home life. The trials of daily living became opportunities to infuse magic into my actions—a moment for gratitude while washing dishes, a spell for abundance spoken over a bubbling pot of stew. Each day felt like a new invitation to let the world slow down and to discover joy in the simplest of tasks.

Becoming a cottage witch is not about perfection but rather a celebration of imperfection and authenticity. It's about creating a nurturing space for yourself and embracing processes that bring you closer to your true self and the magic of the world. This journey has taught me that the true essence of witchcraft resides in the heart—where every act of love, every shared meal, and every moment spent in service to the earth becomes a thread woven into a tapestry of enchantment.

As we venture further into the world of cottage witchery, remember that this path is inherently yours, shaped by your experiences and growth. Each cottage witch has a unique story to tell, and with each chapter, you will explore more dimensions of this enchanting practice. Through understanding, connection, and creativity, the spirit of cottage witchery flourishes, calling us home to ourselves and to the magic that surrounds us.

# Chapter 2: Creating Sacred Space

∞∞∞

Creating sacred space as a cottage witch has been an enchanting journey filled with intention, mindfulness, and connection to the natural world. In my experience, it is the embrace of nature, and that each corner of my home whispers tales of magic and sanctuary.

## Setting the Scene

To begin, I take time to clear out physical clutter, understanding that a tidy space promotes clarity in both mind and spirit. I dust off shelves filled with herbs, crystals, and trinkets collected over time—each item carrying its own story and energy. My home, with its wooden beams and sunlight streaming through the windows, felt alive, ready to host sacred rituals and personal reflection.

## Choosing My Tools

I gather tools that resonate with my practice. A simple altar was set up using a small, rustic table draped with a cloth colored in earthy tones—greens and browns that reflect the garden outside. On this altar, I place a few essential items: a candle to symbolize the element of fire, a bowl of salt for earth's grounding energy, a cup of water representing emotional flow, and a feather for air, encouraging thoughts and communication. Each tool was selected mindfully, each piece grounding me further in my intent.

## Infusing the Space with Intention

Next came the sacred act of cleansing. I walk through my home, holding a bundle of sage, the fragrant smoke swirling around me. As I move from room to room, I speak aloud my intentions, inviting love, protection, and joy into the space. I visualize the energies shifting, the air becoming lighter, filled with possibilities. Essential oils such as lavender and cedar drifted through the air, enhancing the serene atmosphere.

## Creating A Ritual

Once the space feels cleansed and inviting, I craft simple rituals to honor the changing seasons. On the autumn equinox, I adorn my altar with dried leaves, acorns, and a small pumpkin, celebrating the bountiful harvest. As I lit the candle, I reflected on gratitude and abundance, allowing each flame to carry my wishes into the cosmos. The act of creating these seasonal altars has become a cherished tradition.

## Nature as My Ally

Being a cottage witch means staying attuned to the rhythms of nature. I often venture into my garden, gathering fresh herbs, flowers, and stones that call to me. I find solace in the earth, finding beauty in the small things—a blooming flower, the textured bark of a tree, or the gentle rustle of leaves in the wind. Bringing these elements into my sacred space infuses it with energy and life, turning it into a reflection of the world outside.

## Reflection and Growth

As time passes, I've come to understand that creating a sacred space is not a one-time event but a continuous process of growth and adaptation. Each day presents a new opportunity to honor my sacred space, whether through meditation, journaling, or simply enjoying a moment of quiet. It has become a sanctuary that nurtures my spirit and invites inspiration.

Through it all, my practice as a cottage witch has deepened my connection to earth, spirit, and self. My sacred space is not merely an area of my home; it's an embodiment of my inner world, a haven where I can explore, grow, and manifest magic. Each time I enter, I am reminded of the power of intention, the beauty of simplicity, and the endless possibilities that lie within.

## *Creating Sacred Space*

Creating a sacred space in your home is an essential step for anyone wishing to deepen their magical practices. This sanctuary becomes a haven where you can connect with yourself, perform rituals, and invite the energies that align with your intentions. Let's go over how to transform your home into a spiritual retreat, methods for decluttering and cleansing, and rituals to consecrate your sacred space.

### Turning Your Home into a Sanctuary for Magical Practices

Your home is an extension of yourself, and each room contributes to the overall energy of your sanctuary. Begin by selecting a specific area for your sacred space. This could be a corner of a room, a dedicated room, or even a small shrine on a table. Here are some ways to create a sanctuary:

### 1. Choose the Right Location

Select a spot that feels comfortable and private. Ideally, it should be a place where you won't be disturbed, whether by housemates, family members, or pets. Natural light is a bonus, as it enhances the energy of the space.

## 2. Set the Mood

Utilize colors, lighting, and decor to craft the ambiance that resonates with your practices. Softer lighting such as candles or warm-toned lamps can help create a tranquil atmosphere. Decorations should reflect your personal connection to your spirituality:

- **Colors**: Choose colors that resonate with your intentions; blue for calmness and communication, green for healing and growth, red for passion and vitality, etc.
- **Textures**: Incorporate soft fabrics, natural elements like wood or stone, and fountains or plants to enhance the sensory experience.
- **Imagery**: Hang artwork, photographs, or symbols that hold spiritual significance for you, such as mandalas, deity representations, or nature scenes.

## 3. Incorporate Nature

Nature is inherently magical and grounding. You may want to introduce plants, flowers, or stones that resonate with your practice into your space. Consider bringing in elements like:

- **Crystals**: Amethyst for intuition, rose quartz for love, or black tourmaline for protection.
- **Herbs**: Dried herbs in jars or growing herbs in pots can offer both magical and practical benefits.
- **Natural Light**: If possible, let natural light flow into your sacred space. Open curtains during the day to allow sunlight or moonlight to cleanse and energize the area.

**Tips for Decluttering and Cleansing the Space**

A cluttered space can lead to a cluttered mind, making it challenging to connect with the energies you wish to channel. Follow these steps to declutter and cleanse your sacred space effectively:

**1. Declutter with Intent**

Start by removing items that do not serve a purpose or provide joy. Follow the principle of Marie Kondo: if it doesn't spark joy, let it go. Here's how to approach decluttering:

- **Go Item by Item**: Pick up each object and ask yourself if it adds value to your spiritual journey.
- **Create Categories**: Separate items into categories for keeping, donating, repurposing, or discarding.
- **Focus on Functionality**: Only keep tools and materials that are essential to your magical practices. Consider the items you will regularly use and appreciate.

**2. Energetic Cleansing**

Once the clutter is cleared, it's time to cleanse the space energetically. This helps to remove stagnant energy and invites in fresh vibrations. You can choose one or several methods, including:

- **Smoke Cleansing**: Use sage, sweetgrass, or palo santo. Light the herb, allow it to smolder, and waft the smoke around the room while setting intentions for cleansing. Be mindful to open windows to allow negative energy to exit.
- **Salt**: Create a saltwater solution and sprinkle it in the

corners of the space or use it to cleanse objects. Leave a bowl of salt in the area as a protective measure against negativity.

- **Sound**: Use bells, chimes, or singing bowls to raise the vibration of your space. The sound will help break up dense energies and create a harmonious environment.
- **Crystals**: Place selenite or clear quartz around the area to absorb any lingering negative energies.

## *Rituals for Consecrating Your Sacred Space*

Once your space has been thoughtfully selected, decluttered, and cleansed, it's time to consecrate it. This ritual not only formalizes your commitment to the space but infuses it with intention and sacredness.

### 1. Setting Your Intention

Begin by determining the purpose of your sacred space. Will it be used for meditation, spellwork, or divine connection? Creating a clear intention will guide the consecration ritual.

### 2. Gather Your Tools

For your consecration ritual, you may want to gather various items that resonate with you. A few suggestions include:

- Candles (preferably in colors that match your intention)
- Incense or herbs (for smoke cleansing)
- Crystals or other magical items (that you wish to imbue with energy)
- A small bowl for salt or water

- A journal (to record your experience)

## 3. Create a Sacred Circle

Begin by creating a sacred circle around your space. This can be done by placing salt or stones at the perimeter of your space. This circle acts as a barrier against negativity and helps concentrate your energy during the ritual.

## 4. Performing the Ritual

Light your candles and/or incense and find a comfortable seated position within your sacred space. Take a few deep breaths to center yourself. Once you feel grounded, recite affirmations or prayers that resonate with your intention for the space. Here's a sample structure for your ritual:

- **Opening Invocation**: Call upon your guides, deities, or the elements to hold space with you.
- **Consecration Invocation**: Using your hands, visualize white light surrounding the space, and say an invocation like, "I consecrate this space with love and light. May it serve my highest good and be a sanctuary for my practice."
- **Offerings**: You might want to create an offering to honor the energies you've invited in. It could be a simple arrangement of herbs, a small food offering, or a heartfelt note expressing gratitude.
- **Close the Ritual**: Once you feel complete, thank the energies and guides for their presence, extinguish your candles, and ensure your sacred circle is closed.

## 5. Maintenance and Regular Cleansing

To maintain the sacredness of your space, it's essential to visit it regularly. Schedule time for maintenance—perhaps weekly or monthly—for cleansing and recharging the energy. As you deepen your journey, your sacred space will become a reflection of your growth and commitment to your magical practices.

Through conscientious effort, your home can transition into a sacred space that nurtures your spirit and aids your magical endeavors. Embrace the journey as you create a sanctuary where your spirit can thrive and magic can flourish.

# Chapter 3: The Book of Shadows

∞∞∞

The spirit of nature and the elements sang to me, urging me to explore the untamed magic around and within myself. As the seasons transitioned, so did my understanding of the craft, leading me to the transformative endeavor of creating my own Book of Shadows.

It all began on a crisp autumn evening, as the sun dipped below the horizon, painting the sky in mesmerizing hues of orange and deep violet. Mesmerized by the beauty of the fading light, I felt a profound need to document my experiences, thoughts, and the spells I had begun to weave. Until that moment, I had relied on borrowed knowledge—books that lined my shelves and digital blogs that danced across my screen. But I longed for something more personal, a tangible vessel that would hold my journey as I grew in practice.

I set out to create my Book of Shadows with intention, envisioning it as an extension of my spirit and the hearth of my cottage. I gathered materials that resonated with me: smooth brown parchment that felt warm to the touch, a leather-bound cover that was cool yet inviting, and dried herbs that I would press between the pages to capture their essence. Each item felt like a calling, a piece of the universe conspiring to help me express my unique path.

The first page I crafted was an incantation of gratitude, recognizing the spirits of nature that guided me, and the ancestors whose wisdom I've sought. With an ink pen I infused with my own energy; I breathed life into each letter. As I wrote, I found myself in a meditative state, my heart aligned with the beating of the earth, as if the very essence of magic flowed through me.

Over the weeks, each ritual, spell, and herbal correspondence found its place within the pages. I documented my experiences—a homemade candle spell infused with lavender for calm on a restless night, a potion brewed with rose petals to invite love, and the simple joy of collecting wild berries during a sun-drenched afternoon. I illustrated each entry with sketches of herbs and moon phases, adding a personal touch that spoke to my heart's voice, transforming mere words into a sacred tapestry.

One evening, I decided to create a section dedicated to my dreams. I had always been a vivid dreamer, often waking with a sense of lingering magic. I began recording my dreams in detail—searching for hidden messages and symbols, drawing connections to my waking life, and using them as guides in my craft. This reflective practice deepened my connection to my intuition and guided my path forward.

As the seasons turned, my Book of Shadows grew richer in spirit and form. I adorned its cover with beads and twine gathered from my wanderings, symbols imbued with meaning—a crescent moon for intuition, a star for hope, and a circle for unity. Each element encapsulated my growing identity as a cottage witch, rooted in nature and blooming with intention.

On the winter solstice, I felt the culmination of my journey taking shape. The longest night was a time for reflection and release, and I chose to hold a small gathering with friends—a circle of kindred spirits who shared their own paths. We lit candles that flickered like stars against the darkened sky and shared stories of our dreams and aspirations. As the warmth of our laughter wrapped around us like a cozy blanket, I realized that my Book of Shadows was not just a repository of spells but a symbol of community, a manifestation of the energy we create together.

Each time I open its pages now, I am reminded of the journey I took to create it—the lessons learned, and the magic woven into every corner. My Book of Shadows became a beloved companion, my guide through the winding path of witchery that is uniquely mine.

In embracing my cottage witchery, I found not only magic but also a profound connection to myself and the world around me. My Book of Shadows stands as a testament to my growth and the whispers of shadows that beckon me to explore further, reminding me that the greatest magic often lies within the journey itself.

**Concept of a Book of Shadows**

The concept of a Book of Shadows holds a reverent place in the hearts of practitioners of various magical traditions, particularly in Wicca and paganism. It is an essential tool for practitioners, serving as a personal journal of sorts that encapsulates their spiritual journey, knowledge, and practices. Let me review the nature of a Book of Shadows, guide you in creating and personalizing your own, and provide a plethora of page ideas to inspire you in crafting your magical compendium.

**Understanding What a Book of Shadows Is**

A Book of Shadows (often abbreviated as BoS) is more than just a journal; it is a living document that reflects the personal path of the practitioner. Originally, the term is attributed to Gerald Gardner, one of the founders of modern Wicca, who compiled his teachings and rituals into a physical book for his coven. Over time, the concept has evolved, and today, practitioners often use a Book of Shadows to trace their personal experiences, insights, and magickal workings.

The content of a Book of Shadows can vary widely from one individual to another, reflecting their unique beliefs, practices, and personal growth. It may include spells, rituals, correspondences, recipes, and reflections, creating a comprehensive guide that supports the practitioner's spiritual development. More than a handbook, it serves as a vessel for empowerment, a place of reflection, and an archive of one's evolving relationship with the divine.

## How to Create and Personalize Your Own Book of Shadows

Creating your own Book of Shadows is a deeply personal and creative experience. Here are practical steps and considerations to guide you in this journey:

1. **Choose Your Format:**
    - **Physical vs. Digital:** You may prefer a traditional handwritten journal or a digital format. Choose what resonates with you. Physical books allow for handwriting, drawings, and tactile creativity, while digital versions can be easily edited and stored.
    - **Binder vs. Bound Journal:** Some practitioners opt for a three-ring binder to easily add, remove, or rearrange pages, while others cherish the aesthetics of a beautifully bound journal.
2. **Select Your Materials:**
    - If you choose a physical format, invest in quality materials—special journals, decorative paper, or even recycled materials can add meaning.
    - Consider using colored pens, markers, or paint to make your pages visually appealing and reflective of your personality.
3. **Set an Intention:**

- Before you begin writing, take a moment to ground yourself and state your intention for your Book of Shadows. Are you seeking to preserve knowledge, explore spirituality, or document your practices? An intention will guide your writing.

4. **Create an Index or Table of Contents:**
   - This will help you navigate your Book of Shadows easily. Update this section as you add new pages and chapters.

5. **Personalize Your Pages:**
   - Use symbols, stickers, or drawings that resonate with your spiritual practice. Include quotes or passages that inspire you. Your Book of Shadows should reflect your unique energy and intentions.

6. **Incorporate Ritual or Ceremony:**
   - Consider dedicating your Book of Shadows with a small ritual. Light a candle, meditate, or write an affirmation about your commitment to documenting your spiritual journey.

**Page Ideas: Spells, Recipes, Rituals, and Reflections**

Once your Book of Shadows is prepared, it's time to fill it with content. Below are suggestions for what to include:

1. **Spells:**
   - **Simple Spells:** Document spells you've cast, including the intent, materials needed, and steps followed. Include notes on the outcomes and any insights gained.
   - **Correspondences:** Create a section for correspondences (e.g., herbs, colors, planetary associations) that you commonly use in your spells.

- **Original Creations:** Write down any spells you develop yourself, detailing your thought process and the magical theory behind your choices.

2. **Recipes:**

    - **Potions and Brews:** Collect recipes for potions, oils, or incense blends. Include the purpose of each and any specific rituals associated with their use.

    - **Food Recipes:** If you celebrate the Wheel of the Year or specific sabbats with food, compile these recipes alongside blessings or intentions for nourishment.

3. **Rituals:**

    - **Personal Rituals:** Write thorough descriptions of rituals that resonate with you, including altars, tools, and steps. Document personal rituals for the phases of the moon, seasonal changes, or life transitions.

    - **Coven or Group Rituals:** If you participate in rituals with others, capture the essence of these experiences, noting shared prayers or songs.

4. **Reflections:**

    - **Daily Journal:** Create a page for daily or weekly reflections. Write about your experiences, thoughts, feelings, and any revelations you encounter in your practice.

    - **Dream Logs:** Keep a section dedicated to dreams, especially those with vivid messages or imagery. Reflect on how they may relate to your spiritual journey.

    - **Intentions and Goals:** Set and track your intentions and goals within your practice. Reflect periodically on your growth and areas for deeper exploration.

5. **Miscellaneous:**

- **Artwork and Symbols:** Infuse your Book of Shadows with original art or imagery that inspires you. Draw symbols connected with your craft, allowing space for creativity.
- **Meditations and Invocations:** Outline your favorite meditations or invocations for specific deities or energies, including personal insights around them.
- **Books and Resources:** Record a list of books, websites, and other resources that have enriched your practice.

The Book of Shadows is a powerful reflection of your spiritual commitment and personal journey. As you fill its pages, allow it to evolve alongside you—a sacred space for your magick, insights, and knowledge. Personalization is key; the beauty of a Book of Shadows lies in its individuality. Ultimately, this sacred book will not only serve as a record of your experiences but also guide you as you traverse your unique spiritual path. Embrace the journey—every page you create is an invocation of your potent, personal magic.

# Chapter 4: The Elements of Nature

∞∞∞

The natural world is composed of four fundamental elements: Earth, Air, Fire, and Water. These elements are not merely physical substances; they represent powerful archetypal forces that shape our lives, environment, and consciousness. By understanding and honoring these elements, we can deepen our connection to nature and enhance our spiritual practice. Each element's characteristics, associations, and ways to connect and honor them, including rituals that can be integrated into everyday life and organic representations within the home.

**Overview of the Four Elements**

## *Earth*

Earth is the foundation of all physical existence. It embodies stability, nourishment, and strength. Symbolically, Earth represents the physical body, nature, the material world, and the senses. It is associated with abundance, growth, and fertility, reminding us of our connection to the land, our ancestors, and the physical aspects of life.

In various traditions, Earth is linked with the direction of the North and the season of winter. It is often represented by the colors green and brown, and it resonates with the energy of grounding and security. Earth as an element invites us to cultivate gratitude for the physical space we inhabit and the resources we rely on.

## *Air*

Air is the realm of thoughts, ideas, and communication. It reflects the power of intellect, inspiration, and creativity. Air is associated with breath, both literal and metaphorical, serving as a reminder that we are interconnected through the essential act of breathing.

Air is connected to the direction of the East and the season of spring and is often represented by the colors yellow and white. It invites clarity, spontaneity, and new beginnings, symbolizing freedom and the endless possibilities that arise from open-mindedness and exchanges.

## *Fire*

Fire is a transformative force, symbolizing passion, will, and energy. It brings warmth, illumination, and the potential for both destruction and renewal. Fire acts as a purifier; it eliminates what no longer serves, fostering growth and progress.

Fire corresponds to the direction of the South and is associated with summer. It is typically represented by the colors red and orange. Fire's energy encourages us to embrace our desires, take action, and embody our inner strength and courage while also reminding us of the importance of balance to prevent destructive behaviors.

## *Water*

Water embodies the flow of emotions, intuition, and healing. It is associated with transformation, purification, and nourishment, representing the subconscious mind and the emotional landscape of our lives. Water highlights the importance of adaptability, as it changes shape according to its surroundings.

Water is linked to the direction of the West and the season of autumn, represented by the colors blue and silver. As an element, Water encourages us to connect with our emotions, to be fluid in our experiences, and to recognize our interconnectedness with all living beings.

**Connecting with and Honoring Each Element**

**Connecting with Earth**

1. **Grounding Practices**: Spend time outdoors to reinforce your connection with Earth. Walk barefoot on grass or soil; feel the texture beneath your feet. Practice visualization by imagining roots extending from your feet into the ground, anchoring you in the present moment.
2. **Nurturing Rituals**: Create a small garden or tend to houseplants. Celebrate the growth cycle by planting seeds during the spring equinox, nurturing them through care and attention, and giving thanks at harvest.

3. **Earth Offerings**: As a way to honor Earth, offer food scraps, compost, or flowers at the base of a tree, recognizing the cycle of life.

## Connecting with Air

1. **Breathwork and Meditation**: Incorporate breathwork into your meditation routine, focusing on the sensation of air entering and leaving your body. Use this practice to clear your mind and awaken inspiration.
2. **Wind Rituals**: Create an air altar with feathers, incense, or wind chimes. Light some incense outdoors on a breezy day and set the intention to release any stagnant thoughts into the wind.
3. **Gratitude for Communication**: Dedicate time to write letters of gratitude to those who inspire you. Share your thoughts and ideas openly, creating a network of shared wisdom.

## Connecting with Fire

1. **Candle Lightings**: Celebrate significant occasions or intentions by lighting a candle during your rituals. Focus on the flame while visualizing your desires taking shape.
2. **Fire Ceremonies**: Organize small bonfires or use fire pits for releasing what no longer serves you; write down negativity or fear on paper and throw it into the flames.
3. **Passion Projects**: Identify a passion or project ignited by your inner fire and dedicate time to pursuing it. The act of manifestation through creativity is an homage

to the element of Fire.

**Connecting with Water**

1. **Cleansing Rituals**: Use water for spiritual cleansing by taking baths infused with sea salt or essential oils. Visualize the water washing away emotional blockages and inviting clarity.

2. **Moonwater Creation**: Collect rainwater or set a glass bowl of water outside during a full moon, charging it with lunar energy. Use this moonwater for rituals and healing practices.

3. **Fluid Movement**: Engage in activities like swimming or creative dance to honor Water's fluidity, allowing emotions to flow freely. Acknowledge the connection to your intuitive self during these movements.

**Elemental Rituals and Representations in the Home**

Incorporating the elements into your living space can create a harmonious environment that reflects their essence and energy. Here are suggestions on how to manifest each element in your home:

**Earth in the Home**

- **Nature Decor**: Decorate with earthy tones, stones, crystals like clear quartz or hematite, and plants. An indoor garden can serve as a reminder of abundance and grounding.

- **Elemental Altar**: Create a small altar dedicated to Earth using soil, wood, or natural objects. Add symbols representing prosperity and stability, such as coins or blooming plants.

### Air in the Home

- **Open Spaces**: Keep windows open to allow fresh air to circulate. Arrange your furniture to foster open paths for energy to flow.

- **Air Symbols**: Incorporate wind chimes, feathers, or air plants into your decor, adding visual and auditory representations of the Air element.

### Fire in the Home

- **Candle Lighting**: Use candles in your living spaces to create warmth and ambiance. Consider a designated space for lighting candles during intention-setting practices.

- **Dynamic Art**: Use fiery colors like red and orange in your decor; reflect passion and creativity through artwork or textile patterns that invoke the element of Fire.

### Water in the Home

- **Water Features**: Incorporate indoor water features such as aquariums or small fountains. The sound and movement of water create an atmosphere of tranquility and emotional cleansing.

- **Presence of Symbols**: Use blue and silver elements in your decor. Display seashells, driftwood, or images of bodies of water to celebrate this element's soothing quality.

Understanding the four elements—Earth, Air, Fire, and Water—along with honoring their presence in our lives and spaces brings balance, connection, and harmony. By integrating rituals and representations into both our spiritual practices and our homes, we can cultivate a profound sense of belonging within the natural world, becoming custodians of the earth and our emotional journey. Embracing the elements allows us to celebrate the interconnectedness of all life, fostering respect and gratitude for the very fabric of existence.

# Chapter 5: Plant Magic & Herbalism

∞∞∞

In the quiet stillness of nature, amid the bustling sounds of chirping birds and rustling leaves, lies a world of healing, wisdom, and enchantment. For centuries, human beings have turned to the flora that blankets the earth to harness the myriad properties of plants—medicinal, culinary, and magical. This is the essence of herbalism, an ancient practice steeped in both science and tradition. At its heart, herbalism is the study and application of plants for health, wellness, and spiritual connection.

Herbalism operates on the belief that plants possess unique energetic signatures that can align with human needs. This connection allows practitioners to draw not just on the physical benefits of herbs but also the energetic and spiritual qualities that can influence our well-being. When combined with plant magic—a practice that harnesses the energies of plants for spells, rituals, and intentions—a deeper layer of interaction with the natural world unfolds.

Together, herbalism and plant magic form a harmonious dance that celebrates the interdependence of life. Whether for physical healing, emotional support, or spiritual growth, plants whisper their secrets to us, guiding those open to their wisdom.

Let me share how to cultivate a cottage herb garden, discover essential herbs for your garden, delve into their care, and create simple recipes for herbal teas, oils, and salves.

## *Creating a Cottage Herb Garden*

The concept of a cottage herb garden evokes images of charming, untamed gardens overflowing with lush greenery and vibrant blooms. These spaces are not only delightful to behold, but they also serve as sanctuaries of tranquility, healing, and culinary inspiration. When designing your own herb garden, the aim is to create a balanced ecosystem that nurtures both body and spirit.

**Planning Your Space**

1. **Choose the Right Location**: Select a spot that receives at least 4-6 hours of sunlight a day. Herbs thrive in well-drained soil, so avoid areas that tend to hold water or are perpetually shaded.
2. **Garden Design**: Consider using raised beds, containers, or a traditional in-ground garden. A raised bed can provide better drainage and warmer soil, while containers allow for mobility and control over soil conditions.
3. **Soil Preparation**: Amend the garden soil with organic matter, such as compost, to ensure it retains moisture and nutrients. A soil pH between 6.0 and 7.0 is ideal for most culinary herbs.

**Selecting What to Plant**

In your cottage herb garden, aim for a mix of culinary, medicinal, and magical herbs. Here is a list of essential herbs to consider:

- **Basil**: Known for its culinary uses and reputed to attract love and prosperity.

- **Thyme**: Excellent for cooking and believed to boost courage and purification.
- **Rosemary**: A versatile culinary herb with associations of remembrance and protection.
- **Lavender**: Known for its calming properties, it invites tranquility and peace.
- **Sage**: Widely used for cleansing rituals, it is also beneficial for digestion.
- **Peppermint**: Refreshing for tea and digestion and thought to promote clarity and wisdom.
- **Chamomile**: A soothing herb for tea and sleep, associated with peace and relaxation.
- **Yarrow**: Often used for its healing properties, it has strong protective and divinatory associations.

## Care Instructions

Proper maintenance ensures a bountiful herb garden:

1. **Watering**: Herbs generally prefer soil that is kept slightly moist. Water early in the morning or late in the afternoon to minimize evaporation. Be cautious of overwatering, as many herbs dislike soggy roots.
2. **Pruning and Harvesting**: Regular trimming encourages bushier growth. Harvest leaves as needed but avoid cutting more than one-third of the plant at once. This practice helps maintain the plant's vigor.
3. **Weed Control**: Keep the garden tidy by removing weeds, which can compete for nutrients and water. Hand-pulling is often the most effective and least disruptive method.
4. **Pest Management**: Observe plants for signs of pests or ailments. Use organic insecticidal soap or neem oil as a

gentle remedy for infestations.
5. **Seasonal Care**: In cooler climates, many herbs will die back in winter. Some can be brought indoors, while others may be harvested and dried for later use.

## *Creating an Herbal Apothecary*

In the heart of every cottage witch lies an intimate connection with the natural world, a bond that draws from the healing wonders of plants and herbs. An herbal apothecary serves as a sacred sanctuary, a place of magic and healing where one can store, prepare, and work with nature's bounty. Don't worry I will guide you through the process of creating your very own herbal apothecary at home, blending practical knowledge with magical intention.

**Understanding Your Intentions**

Before embarking on the journey of building your herbal apothecary, take a moment to reflect on your intentions. What do you hope to achieve with your apothecary? Is it for personal health, spiritual growth, natural remedies for your family, or creating magical potions and charms? Understanding your intentions will help shape the space, the herbs you choose, and how you incorporate them into your life.

## *Step 1: Establishing Your Space*

Your herbal apothecary doesn't require an elaborate or extensive setup; it can flourish in a small space or even a corner of your kitchen.

**Choosing the Location**

Consider a quiet, dedicated space in your home that resonates with you. Ideal spots include:

- **A kitchen counter:** Accessible for daily cooking and herbal preparation.
- **A cozy shelf:** A bookcase or a decorative shelf in your living space.
- **A dedicated table:** An altar where you can perform rituals and blend herbs.

Ensure the location has good light, preferably natural, as this fosters growth and vitality in your herbs.

**Creating the Atmosphere**

Infuse your space with an inviting ambiance. Use natural materials—wood, glass, and stone—and adorn the area with elements like candles, crystals, or an incense holder. Personal touches such as artwork, photographs, or talismans can enhance the energy.

## *Step 2: Gathering Your Tools and Containers*

To craft your apothecary, you'll need an array of tools and containers that are both functional and harmonious with your aesthetic.

### *Essential Tools*

1. **Mortar and Pestle:** Essential for grinding dried herbs and preparing tea blends.
2. **Scissors or Herb Shears:** To harvest fresh herbs and cut dried leaves.

3. **Measuring Spoons and Cups:** For precise herbal measurements, especially in potions and tinctures.
4. **Scale:** A small kitchen scale for accurate measurements, especially with larger batches.
5. **Funnel:** To pour liquids without spilling, especially useful for tinctures and oils.
6. **Labels and Markers:** To note the name and properties of your herbs.

## Choosing Containers

Containers should ideally be glass or wooden to retain the energy of the herbs:

- **Jars:** Glass jars (mason jars work great) for storing dried herbs.
- **Bottles:** Dark glass bottles for oils and tinctures to protect from light.
- **Cloth Bags:** Breathable storage for bulk herbs to allow them to maintain integrity.

Consider organizing your herbs alphabetically or by virtue (e.g., medicinal, culinary, magical) for easy access.

## *Step 3: Sourcing Herbs*

### Harvesting Wild Herbs

If you are fortunate to live in an area rich in flora, you may forage for wild herbs. Before foraging, ensure you are knowledgeable about the plants in your area—both their identifying features and their uses. Key herbs to consider for your apothecary include:

- **Chamomile:** Calming and soothing.
- **Yarrow:** Great for first aid.
- **St. John's Wort:** Known for its antidepressant properties.

Always practice ethical foraging—take only what you need and ensure you have permission to gather from private lands.

**Buying Quality Herbs**

If foraging isn't an option, consider purchasing herbs from reputable sources. Look for bulk herb shops, apothecaries, or online retailers specializing in organic, sustainably sourced herbs. When buying, choose:

- **Dried Herbs:** Ensure they are stored in cool, dark conditions.
- **Fresh Herbs:** Opt for organic from farmer's markets or local stores.

**Growing Your Own Herbs**

There is no substitute for freshness, and growing your own herbs is a rewarding experience. Consider creating a small garden or using containers for:

- **Basil:** A wonderful culinary and magical herb.
- **Mint:** Versatile for teas and potions.
- **Lavender:** Calming and aromatic, perfect for sachets.

## *Step 4: Common Herbs and Their Uses*

As your collection grows, familiarize yourself with the properties of commonly used herbs. Here are a few staples to include in your apothecary:

- **Peppermint:** Digestive aid, energizing in spell work.
- **Rosemary:** Supports memory, protection in magic.
- **Echinacea:** Immune booster, useful in tinctures.
- **Sage:** Cleansing herb, great for smudging and purification rituals.

Create an herbal correspondences notebook containing descriptions, properties, and uses of your herbs for reference and inspiration.

## *Step 5: Preparing Herbal Remedies*

With your apothecary set up, you can start creating various herbal remedies:

### Herbal Teas

1. **Choose Your Herbs:** Select one or more dried herbs.
2. **Measure:** Use about 1 tsp of dried herb per cup of water.
3. **Infuse:** Pour hot water over the herbs and steep for 5-10 minutes.
4. **Strain and Enjoy:** Use a fine strainer to remove the herbs.

### Tinctures

1. **Fill a Jar:** Halfway with chopped fresh herbs or 1/4 full with dried herbs.

2. **Add Alcohol:** Fill with vodka or brandy until the herbs are submerged.
3. **Seal and Store:** Place in a dark cupboard for 4-6 weeks, shaking gently.
4. **Strain:** After the infusion period, strain and bottle the liquid.

**Herbal Oils**

1. **Choose Your Base Oil:** Olive oil, almond oil, or jojoba work well.
2. **Fill a Jar:** With herbs, covering them with oil.
3. **Infuse:** Let the mixture sit in a warm place for several weeks, shaking daily.
4. **Strain:** When ready, strain and bottle, using for topical applications or spellwork.

## *Step 6: Incorporating Magick*

As a cottage witch, your herbal apothecary can be a powerful magical tool. Intention is key. Whether crafting potions for love, healing, protection, or prosperity, infuse your spells and remedies with focused intention and visualization.

**Creating Herbal Charms and Sachets**

- **Choose Your Intent:** Define a clear intention for your charm or sachet.
- **Select Herbs:** Based on their properties that align with your goal.
- **Craft the Charm:** Blend the herbs and fill a small bag or cloth.

- **Charge with Intention:** Hold the sachet, envision your intention coming to life, and say a few words of power.

**Your Journey Awaits**

Creating an herbal apothecary is not just about gathering herbs; it's about forging a deeper connection with nature and yourself. It is a journey of learning, healing, and practicing your craft. As you gather your herbs and concoct your remedies, remember that every preparation is infused with your energy, making each creation uniquely yours. Embrace the power of plants, allow them into your magical practice, and watch as your herbal apothecary flourishes, bridging the gap between the beauty of nature and the art of witchcraft.

**Simple Herbal Recipes for Teas, Oils, and Salves**

Harnessing the power of herbs can be a profoundly rewarding experience. Below are simple recipes that illustrate how to transform your garden bounty into delightful homemade remedies.

# Herbal Teas

## Calming Chamomile Tea

- **Ingredients**: 1 tablespoon dried chamomile flowers, 1 cup boiling water, honey (optional).
- **Instructions**: Place chamomile flowers in a teapot or infuser. Pour boiling water over them and let steep for 5-7 minutes. Strain if using loose flowers, sweeten with honey if desired, and enjoy.

## Refreshing Mint Tea

- **Ingredients**: 1 tablespoon fresh peppermint leaves, 1 cup boiling water, lemon (optional).
- **Instructions**: Place peppermint in your teapot or cup, pour boiling water over leaves, and steep for 5-10 minutes. Add a slice of lemon for a zesty twist.

# Herbal Oils

## Infused Rosemary Oil

- **Ingredients**: 1 cup olive oil, ½ cup fresh rosemary.
- **Instructions**: Place rosemary in a clean jar and cover with olive oil. Seal and place in a sunny spot for 1-2 weeks, shaking gently every couple of days. After infusing, strain out the herbs and store the oil in a dark glass bottle.

## Lavender-Infused Oil

- **Ingredients**: 1 cup grapeseed or almond oil, ½ cup dried lavender buds.
- **Instructions**: Combine oil and lavender in a double boiler over low heat for 1-2 hours. Alternatively, you can place the mixture in a jar and set it in a sunny window for 2 weeks. Strain and store your fragrant oil in a glass jar.

# Herbal Salves

## Healing Herbal Salve

- **Ingredients**: ¼ cup infused olive oil (from the rosemary or lavender recipe), 2 tablespoons beeswax.
- **Instructions**: In a double boiler, melt the beeswax and infused oil together until fully combined. Pour into small containers and allow to cool and set. This salve can be used for minor scrapes, dryness, or as a comforting balm for tired muscles.

## Soothing Chamomile Salve

- **Ingredients**: ¼ cup chamomile-infused oil, 2 tablespoons beeswax, optional essential oils (lavender or tea tree).
- **Instructions**: Similar to the healing salve, melt beeswax with chamomile oil in a double boiler until combined. Pour into tins and cool. The addition of lavender or tea tree essential oil can enhance its calming or antiseptic properties.

As you embark on your journey into plant magic and herbalism, remember that each herb carries its own lessons—about patience, nurturing, and the profound connections that exist between all living things. Your cottage herb garden is not merely a collection of plants; it is a sanctuary of healing, creativity, and magic. By tending to these verdant allies with love and intention, you weave a tapestry of health and well-being that nourishes both body and soul.

# Chapter 6: Seasonal Celebrations & Sabbats

∞∞∞

In the heart of cottage witchery lies a profound reverence for the cyclical nature of life, as embodied in the Wheel of the Year. This ancient concept consists of a series of eight festivals known as Sabbats, each marking a significant point in the seasonal cycle. Rooted in the agricultural practices of our ancestors, these celebrations honor the changing seasons and the rhythms of nature, aligning a witch's spiritual practices with the world around them. The Wheel of the Year serves as a reminder of the interconnectedness of all living things and encourages practitioners to live in harmony with nature.

The eight Sabbats, which include Samhain, Yule, Imbolc, Ostara, Beltane, Litha, Lammas, and Mabon, each present their unique energy and themes. For cottage witches, these dates are not merely markers in time but opportunities to deepen their connection with the Earth and fortify their personal and communal traditions.

## The Eight Sabbats

1. **Samhain (October 31 - November 1)**: Considered the witch's New Year, Samhain is a time when the veil between the worlds is thinnest, allowing for

communion with ancestors and spirits. It marks the end of the harvest season and the onset of winter.

2. **Yule (Winter Solstice)**: Celebrated around December 21, Yule honors the rebirth of the Sun. This Sabbat is a time for reflection, rest, and rekindling the inner light.

3. **Imbolc (February 1-2)**: A festival of light and purification, Imbolc celebrates the first stirrings of spring and honors the goddess Brigid. It symbolizes awakening and the potential for growth.

4. **Ostara (Spring Equinox)**: Occurring around March 21, Ostara celebrates balance, fertility, and the return of life. It encourages acts of renewal and planting new ideas and intentions.

5. **Beltane (May 1)**: A fire festival that marks the height of spring and the onset of summer. Beltane is a time of passion, creativity, and fertility, celebrated with bonfires and maypole dances.

6. **Litha (Summer Solstice)**: The longest day of the year, Litha, around June 21, is a celebration of abundance, growth, and the power of the Sun at its zenith. It is a time of joy and abundance.

7. **Lammas (August 1)**: Celebrated as the first harvest, Lammas acknowledges gratitude for the earth's bounty. Traditionally, loaves of bread made from the new grain are shared as a symbol of sustenance and community.

8. **Mabon (Autumn Equinox)**: Occurring around September 21, Mabon is a time of Thanksgiving for the harvest. It marks the balance of light and dark and invites reflection and gratitude.

Together, these Sabbats create a continuum that provides a framework for personal growth, community bonding, and the celebration of life's cyclical nature.

## Rituals and Traditions for Celebrating Each Sabbat

### Samhain Rituals

- **Honoring Ancestors**: Set up an ancestor altar with photographs, mementos, and offerings of food or drink. Light a candle for each ancestor as a way to invite their presence.
- **Divination**: Utilize tarot cards, scrying, or other divination tools to gain insight into the coming year.

### Yule Rituals

- **Yule Log**: On the night of the solstice, bring a Yule log into your home. Decorate it with natural items such as pinecones, holly, or herbs. As it burns, make a wish for the year ahead.
- **Feasting and Reflection**: Prepare a feast featuring seasonal foods. As you dine, share stories or intentions for renewal.

### Imbolc Rituals

- **Candle Ritual**: Light candles to symbolize the returning light. For a stronger connection, write your hopes and wishes on small pieces of paper and place them beneath the candles.
- **Cleansing**: Perform a deep cleaning of your space to symbolize the purification and welcome in fresh energy.

### Ostara Rituals

- **Egg Decorating**: Create decorated eggs to symbolize

fertility and new beginnings. Engage in a small egg hunt as a fun way to celebrate rebirth.

- **Planting Seeds**: Use this time to plant seeds—both literal in your garden and metaphorical by setting intentions for future growth.

## Beltane Rituals

- **Bonfire Ritual**: Celebrate by lighting a bonfire, around which you can dance, sing, and share blessings. Jump over the fire to symbolize purification and commitment to your goals.
- **Flower Crowns**: Create flower crowns to wear during celebrations. Flowers symbolize the blossoming of life and the fertility of the land.

## Litha Rituals

- **Nature Walk**: Immerse yourself in the energy of the season by taking a nature walk. Collect herbs, flowers, and other gifts from the earth, creating an offering to leave in gratitude.
- **Sun Celebration**: Create a shrine to honor the Sun. Include solar symbols, candles, and elements to celebrate the abundance present in your life.

## Lammas Rituals

- **Bread Making**: Bake bread using the first grains of the season and share it with family and friends as an offering of gratitude.
- **Harvest Festival**: Host a gathering to celebrate the harvest. Share stories, food, and blessings for abundance.

**Mabon Rituals**

- **Gratitude Ceremony**: Hold a simple gratitude ceremony where you write down what you are thankful for from the harvest season and what you aim to manifest in the new cycle.// 
- **Feast of Sharing**: Prepare a feast with seasonal produce, inviting friends or family to partake in the fruits of your labor.

**How to Create Seasonal Altars and Decorations**

Creating seasonal altars not only personalizes your practice but also invites the energy of each Sabbat into your home.

**General Guidelines for Seasonal Altars**

1. **Base Structure**: Choose a flat surface—such as a table or shelf—as your altar space. Cover it with a cloth that reflects the season or desired color.
2. **Nature's Offerings**: Incorporate items from nature, such as stones, leaves, flowers, and twigs, which resonate with the current season.
3. **Representative Symbols**: Use symbols that represent each Sabbat. For example, during Yule, incorporate evergreen branches or candles; during Ostara, use eggs and pastel colors.
4. **Candles and Light**: Utilize candles in colors associated with the season (white, green, gold for Yule; orange and black for Samhain, etc.). Light them during rituals for added power and atmosphere.
5. **Crystals**: Select crystals that correspond with the energy of each season to amplify intention and focus during rituals. For instance, rose quartz during Imbolc

for love and self-care, or garnet during Litha for vitality.

**Seasonal Decorations**

- **Samhain**: Adorn your space with pumpkins, gourds, and black and orange colors. Hang images of bats or skeletons to symbolize the thinning veil.
- **Yule**: Decorate with evergreen boughs, cinnamon, star anise, and symbols of the Sun, such as suns or bright ornaments.
- **Imbolc**: Incorporate white and golden colors, along with candles mimicking the light of the returning Sun. Use snowdrops or other early spring flowers.
- **Ostara**: Add pastel colors and egg motifs. Place small baskets of seeds or live plants on your altar.
- **Beltane**: Decorate with flowers, ribbons, and across the altar, including symbols of fertility like rabbits or the Beltane fire.
- **Litha**: Use sun symbols, yellow and gold colors, and fresh herbs or flowers to evoke growth and vitality.
- **Lammas**: Display sheaves of wheat, corn, and harvest bounty to celebrate the first fruits of labor.
- **Mabon**: Decorate with autumn leaves, acorns, and symbols of balance, such as scales.

Through these rituals, decorations, and the celebration of the Sabbats, cottage witches can develop a deeper connection to nature and its rhythms. Engaging fully with each season invites a sense of wonder, gratitude, and continuity, and fosters a nurturing environment in which all beings can thrive. The Wheel of the Year reminds us that life is a sacred cycle of death and rebirth, and as we honor these cycles, we align ourselves more closely with the magic of the Earth.

# Chapter 7: Kitchen Witchery

∞∞∞

In the heart of every home lies the kitchen, a sacred space where alchemy happens daily. It is here that humble ingredients transform into nourishment, and with a sprinkle of intention and inflection of enchantment, they can also become powerful conduits for magic. Kitchen witchery embraces the art of cooking not just as a sustenance endeavor but as a spiritual practice that intertwines culinary creativity with magical intention. Let's go over the harmonious intersection of cooking and magic, providing recipes infused with purpose, and guiding you in establishing a magical kitchen equipped with essential tools, herbs, and enriching routines.

**The Intersection of Cooking and Magic**

At its core, the practice of kitchen witchery celebrates the mundane as divine. Cooking has always been intrinsic to well-being, family, and community; it's an act of love and care. By integrating magic into this daily ritual, practitioners can elevate the act of cooking to a form of spiritual expression.

**Intention** is at the crux of kitchen witchery. When preparing meals, one can set intentions that resonate with the desired energy one wishes to manifest in their life. This could range from invoking love, safety, health, prosperity, or healing. A simple task like chopping vegetables can become a meditative ritual—visualizing nurturing energy infusing each cut—and the results can yield not only a meal but a potion of intention.

Like any craft, kitchen witchery draws from personal symbolism and heritage. Different cultures and traditions provide varied insights. In some practices, herbs are used not only for flavor but also for their properties, serving dual purposes. Foods themselves carry their own magical correspondences: for instance, garlic can ward off negativity, and honey symbolizes abundance. Understanding these relationships can deepen the magical dimension of food preparation.

**Recipes Infused with Intention and Spellwork**

The practice of kitchen witchery is richly varied and deeply personal. Recipes here transcend standard preparations; they invite intention, spellwork, and spiritual focus. Below are a few recipes designed to align with specific magical goals. Feel free to personalize them to suit your particular craft and intuition.

## *1. Love Infusion Tea*

**Intention:** To attract and enhance love in your life.

**Ingredients:**

- 1 teaspoon dried rose petals (for love)
- 1 teaspoon dried hibiscus (to attract)
- 1 teaspoon chamomile (for harmony)
- 2 cups water
- Honey (optional, for sweetness and to symbolize attraction)

**Instructions:**

1. Begin by grounding yourself. Hold the dry herbs in your hands, closing your eyes and visualizing your intention for love infusing each petal.
2. Bring the water to a gentle boil in a pot. As it heats, repeat your desired affirmation, such as "Love flows freely into my life."
3. Place the herbs in a tea strainer or directly into the boiling water. Allow them to steep for 5-7 minutes, imagining the herbs releasing their properties.
4. Strain into a cup, sweeten with honey if desired, and savor the tea while reflecting on the love you are inviting into your life.

## *2. Protection Soup*

**Intention:** To create a protective barrier around your home or loved ones.

**Ingredients:**

- 1 onion, chopped (for protection)
- 2 cloves garlic, minced (to ward off negativity)
- 1 cup carrots, chopped (for stability)
- 1 cup celery, chopped (for healing)
- 4 cups vegetable or chicken broth
- Salt and pepper to taste
- A few sprigs of fresh rosemary (for protection)

**Instructions:**

1. In a warm pot, administer gratitude for the ingredients you are about to use, acknowledging their roots in the earth.
2. Sauté the onion and garlic until translucent. Visualize

a white light surrounding your cooking space, adding layers of protection.

3. Add the carrots and celery, stirring them while stating your intention for safety.
4. Pour in the broth, season with salt and pepper, and bring the mixture to a boil, then simmer for 20 minutes.
5. Add rosemary at the end and stir in your protective intent.
6. Serve the soup in bowls, setting the intention that it will shield and bless those consuming it.

## *3. Prosperity Bread*

**Intention:** To invite abundance into your life.

**Ingredients:**

- 2 cups of flour (for the foundation)
- 1 tablespoon sugar (to sweeten abundance)
- 1 teaspoon salt (for balance)
- 2 teaspoons yeast (to raise your intentions)
- 1 cup warm water
- Olive oil (for blessings on your financial ventures)

**Instructions:**

1. Begin by cleansing your space—light a candle or burn incense.
2. In a bowl, combine warm water and yeast, allowing it to proof. During this time, envision your financial goals as tangible fruits.
3. In another bowl, mix flour, sugar, and salt, forming a circle as a symbol of wholeness and completion.

4. Combine the wet and dry ingredients, kneading the dough while chanting a prosperity affirmation such as "My paths are paved in abundance."
5. Let the dough rise in a warm place for an hour, visualizing the tangible results of your hard work expanding as it does.
6. Preheat the oven as the dough rises. Shape the bread and brush it lightly with olive oil before baking until golden — let the scent infuse the air with abundance.

**Creating a Magical Kitchen: Tools, Herbs, and Routines**

To embrace kitchen witchery fully, establishing a sacred cooking space is essential. This isn't merely about physical appearance but rather infusing your kitchen with intention, tools, and herbs that resonate with your magical practice.

## *Essential Tools*

1. **Wand or Wooden Spoon:** Use a wand made from a branch of a tree that resonates with your intention or a wooden spoon you consider sacred. Both can stir both your pot and your intention.
2. **Mortar and Pestle:** For grinding herbs and spices, this tool embodies the essence of alchemy—transforming the mundane into the magical.
3. **Cauldron or Pot:** A pot serves as a vessel for both cooking and ritual. An iron cauldron can be particularly symbolic.
4. **Whisk or Mixing Bowl:** These can be used for both mundane cooking and ritual blends, enhancing the energy as you mix.

## *Magical Herbs*

Curate a selection of herbs that resonate with your magical intents. Here is a non-exhaustive list:

- **Basil:** Prosperity and protection.
- **Sage:** Cleansing and purification.
- **Cinnamon:** Attraction and prosperity.
- **Mint:** Vitality and inspiration.
- **Thyme:** Strength and courage.
- **Rosemary:** Protection and remembrance.

Ensure these herbs are stored in a respectful manner—preferably in glass containers labeled according to their purpose. Take a moment before using each herb to meditate on its energy and how it aligns with your intention.

## *Routines and Rituals*

Incorporate daily and seasonal routines that deepen your magical connection with cooking. Here are a few suggestions:

1. **Daily Altar:** Create a small altar in your kitchen with offerings of herbs, crystals, and personal charms that inspire your culinary magic.
2. **Moon Phases:** Align your cooking practices with lunar cycles, preparing specific dishes that correspond with the moon phases—full moon for abundance recipes, new moon for manifestation dishes.
3. **Gratitude Practices:** Before each meal, practice gratitude—acknowledge the earth, laborers, and the transformation that has occurred in your kitchen.

4. **Cooking that Tells a Story:** Use inherited recipes or create new ones that tell your family's story or narratives that resonate with your heart—stirring in the essence of your lineage.

As you embark on your kitchen witchery journey, remember that success lies not in perfection but in the love and energy you pour into your culinary creations. Whether you're baking a loaf of bread or brewing a cup of tea, every act can be an incantation, a moment to weave magic into the fabric of your everyday life. Allow your kitchen to be the enchanted space that nurtures not only your body but your spirit, manifesting the magic you wish to create in the world around you.

# Chapter 8: Moon Magic

∞∞∞

As ancient as the tides that ebb and flow beneath her embrace, the moon has been a symbol of mystery, intuition, and change throughout human history. It has inspired countless myths, rituals, and magical practices. I want to review the fascinating world of moon magic, exploring the lunar phases, the rituals that harness lunar energy, and the tools that you can create to amplify your magical workings.

**Understanding Lunar Phases and Their Influence on Magic**

The moon transitions through eight distinct phases, each imbued with unique energies that can significantly influence magical practices. Understanding these phases allows practitioners to align their intentions with the moon's rhythm, enhancing the potency of their spells and rituals.

## *The Lunar Phases*

1. **New Moon**: The beginning of the lunar cycle, symbolizing new beginnings, potential, and intentions. This is the ideal time for setting intentions, initiating projects, and planting the seeds of what you wish to manifest.
2. **Waxing Crescent**: As the moon begins to grow, so

does your energy. This phase is perfect for encouraging growth in your endeavors. Focus on spells that promote development, attraction, and increase.

3. **First Quarter**: A time to take decisive action. The moon's light is strong, and this is an excellent moment for overcoming obstacles and affirming your intentions.

4. **Waxing Gibbous**: The moon is nearing fullness, and energies are building. Use this time to fine-tune your goals and prepare for culminating actions.

5. **Full Moon**: The peak of lunar energy. A time of abundance, illumination, and completion. Full moons are particularly powerful for manifestations, divination, and rituals aimed at achieving desires.

6. **Waning Gibbous**: As the moon begins to wane, it's a time of gratitude and reflection. Use this phase to release what no longer serves you and to assess the manifestations of your recent intentions.

7. **Last Quarter**: In this phase, a deeper release is required. It's a time for letting go and making space for new growth in the next cycle. Perform banishing spells and rituals, cleansing negative influences from your life.

8. **Waning Crescent**: The final phase before the New Moon, this is a time for rest and recuperation, allowing you to reflect on your past intentions and prepare for the new cycle ahead.

Understanding these phases not only provides guidance for your magical practice but also helps cultivate a deeper relationship with the natural world, recognizing the cycles of life, death, and rebirth mirrored in our own experiences.

### Moon Rituals for Manifesting and Releasing

Harnessing the moon's energy is an integral part of many magical practices. Below are examples of rituals tailored for both manifesting during the New Moon and releasing during the Full Moon.

## *New Moon Manifestation Ritual*

**Purpose:** Set clear intentions for the month ahead.

**Materials Needed:**
- A quiet space
- A small bowl of water
- A piece of paper and a pen
- A candle (preferably white or silver)
- Crystals associated with new beginnings (e.g., moonstone, clear quartz)

**Steps:**
1. **Prepare the Space**: Cleanse your area with sage or your preferred method. Arrange your materials mindfully.
2. **Center Yourself**: Light the candle, sit comfortably, and take deep breaths to relax. Focus your energy inward.
3. **Write Your Intentions**: On the piece of paper, write down your intentions or goals clearly and positively, as if they are already happening.
4. **Energize the Water**: Hold the bowl of water in your hands and visualize your intentions flowing into the water. Understand that this water will serve as a vessel, holding your intentions.
5. **Seal the Intentions**: Fold the paper that contains

your intentions and place it under the bowl. Feel the intentions beneath the water and light illuminating them.

6. **Close the Ritual**: Thank the moon for its energy, blow out the candle, and let the water sit overnight. The following day, you may choose to bury the paper or keep it in a sacred space as a reminder of your intentions.

## *Full Moon Release Ritual*

**Purpose:** Let go of negativity, fears, or unhealthy patterns.

**Materials Needed:**

- A quiet place outdoors or by a window to see the moon
- A piece of paper and a pen
- A fire-safe bowl or container
- A black candle
- Salt (for purification)
- Crystals for release (e.g., obsidian, black tourmaline)

**Steps:**

1. **Create Sacred Space**: Begin by cleansing your space with salt or incense. Set up your materials where the full moonlight can shine upon you.
2. **Light the Black Candle**: This represents your intention to release negative energies. Focus on the flame and visualize your burdens being burnt away.
3. **Write Down What to Release**: On the paper, write down anything you wish to let go of—fears, bad habits, toxic relationships.

4. **Symbolic Burning**: One by one, hold each intention near the candle flame and chant: "As I release this, I am free." Once it catches fire, place it in the fire-safe bowl, watching it burn completely.
5. **Express Gratitude**: Thank the full moon for its illuminating power, releasing what no longer serves you, and welcoming in freshness.
6. **Ground Yourself**: After the ritual, clear any residual energy by walking around outdoors barefoot or meditating on feelings of freedom and lightness.

## Crafting Moon Water and Other Lunar Tools

One of the most accessible forms of moon magic involves creating moon water—charged water that harnesses the moon's energy, ideal for infusing into your magical workings, rituals, cleansing baths, or daily life.

### *Crafting Moon Water*

**Materials Needed:**
- A clean glass jar or bowl
- Purified water (spring, filtered, or distilled)
- Crystals (optional, e.g., clear quartz, amethyst)
- A piece of cloth or lid

**Steps:**
1. **Prepare Your Container**: Rinse the jar or bowl with salt water to cleanse it and set your intention for the moon water.
2. **Fill with Water**: Pour purified water into the container, leaving some space at the top.
3. **Charge Under the Moonlight**: Place the container

outside or by a window where it can receive moonlight. Allow it to sit under the moon, preferably from the night of the Full Moon or during the New Moon.

4. **Infuse with Intent**: While the water charges, visualize your intentions merging with the water. You can add crystals to amplify the energy as they soak in the lunar light.
5. **Seal and Store**: Once the moon has set or you feel ready, seal your jar with a cloth or lid. Store it in a dark, cool place.

## *Creating Other Lunar Tools*

**Moon Oil**: Combine carrier oils with essential oils that resonate with the intention you desire (e.g., lavender for calm, bergamot for joy) and let them sit under the moon to charge. Use this oil for anointing candles or your pulse points during rituals.

**Moon Journal**: Dedicate a journal to record your lunar observations, intentions, and magical practices. Reflect on your emotional experiences and use it to track your manifestations over the lunar cycles.

**Moon Amulets**: Create magical talismans using items collected under the moonlight or infused with moon energy. This could include crystals, herbs, or charms. Each item should resonate with specific intentions — protection, love, success, etc.

Moon magic offers a unique opportunity to connect with the rhythms of nature, harnessing the potent energy of the lunar phases to support your magical intentions. By understanding the moon's phases, performing both manifestation and release rituals, and crafting lunar tools like moon water, you can deepen your practice and align your intentions with the cycles of the universe. Embrace the wisdom of the moon, and let her guiding light illuminate your path on this journey of personal and spiritual growth.

# Chapter 9: Crystals & Gemstones

∞∞∞

Crystals and gemstones are not merely beautiful objects; they are potent tools in the practice of cottage witchery. Tapping into the earth's treasures can enhance your craft, promote well-being, and create a harmonious living environment. How we choose and work with crystals unique to cottage witchery, how to cleanse, charge, and program these stones, and how to incorporate them into your everyday life and home decor.

**Choosing and Working with Crystals Unique to Cottage Witchery**

In cottage witchery, the selection of crystals is often guided by personal intuition, the specific energies sought, and local availability. Here are a few crystals that resonate particularly well with the cottage witch ethos:

### *Amethyst*

Amethyst is a beautiful violet crystal that has long been associated with spirituality, intuition, and tranquility. Known as the stone of sobriety, it has been used throughout history to prevent intoxication and promote clarity of mind. For cottage witches, amethyst can enhance meditation practices and deepen one's connection to the divine. Its calming energy makes it an excellent tool for ritual work, particularly during moon phases that encourage reflection and emotional healing. Placing amethyst in your sacred space can help create an atmosphere conducive to peaceful contemplation and spiritual growth.

In practical use, amethyst is often utilized for protection against negative energies and psychic attacks. It can also be employed in divination practices, providing clarity and insight during readings. For witches who practice dream work, amethyst is known to enhance dream recall and promote vivid dreams, making it a useful ally for understanding subconscious messages. Additionally, this powerful stone can be incorporated into spellwork for emotional balance, promoting feelings of calm and joy, and guiding practitioners through difficult emotional transitions.

## *Rose Quartz*

Known as the stone of unconditional love, rose quartz embodies compassion, warmth, and emotional healing. It resonates deeply with the heart chakra, allowing cottage witches to cultivate love not just for themselves but also for others and the world around them. Rose quartz can be used in spells and rituals to attract love, friendship, and harmony into one's life. It's particularly effective for fostering self-love and emotional healing, making it an invaluable companion during times of personal struggles or grief. A simple yet powerful practice involves laying a piece of rose quartz on your chest during meditation to enhance feelings of love and acceptance.

In addition to its love-associated properties, rose quartz is also beneficial for enhancing emotional balance. It can help soothe anxieties and fears, making it a perfect stone for those engaging in shadow work or personal growth. Practitioners often include rose quartz in crystal grids or carry it in their pockets to maintain a calming and loving energy throughout the day. Whether placed on an altar or used during healing rituals, rose quartz reminds witches of the importance of love and compassion both in their practice and their daily lives.

## Black Tourmaline

Black tourmaline is revered among cottage witches for its protective qualities and grounding energy. This potent stone is known for its ability to repel negative energies and protect its wearer from psychic attacks and electromagnetic radiation. For witches seeking to create a safe and tranquil space for their craft, black tourmaline is an essential component of any crystal collection. It can be placed near electronic devices to absorb harmful energies or positioned at the corners of one's property to create a protective barrier. This grounding stone helps to balance energy and can assist in achieving a centered state of mind during rituals or meditation.

Moreover, black tourmaline can be utilized in transformation spells and rituals aimed at releasing negativity or unproductive thought patterns. It encourages self-healing and emotional resilience, making it a valuable ally during challenging times. Cottage witches often incorporate black tourmaline into spells designed for banishing negativity and attracting positive energy. By working with this stone, practitioners can cultivate an atmosphere of safety and security, allowing them to focus on their intentions and magical workings without unwanted distractions.

## Citrine

Citrine is a vibrant yellow crystal known for its association with abundance, prosperity, and personal power. As a stone that resonates with the solar plexus chakra, it encourages confidence, creativity, and motivation. Cottage witches can harness citrine's uplifting energy to manifest goals, attract financial opportunities, and energize their manifestations. This stone is particularly useful during the new moon when setting intentions for growth and prosperity. By placing citrine on an altar or carrying it during business endeavors, one can invoke its supportive energy to empower actions towards desired outcomes.

Beyond its prosperity attributes, citrine is also celebrated for its ability to enhance mental clarity and dispel negativity. It aids in overcoming self-doubt and fear, facilitating clearer decision-making and enhancing one's ability to take action. Witchcraft practices may involve using citrine in ritual work to stimulate joy and optimism, fostering a positive mindset. Additionally, it's often integrated into spells targeting personal growth, motivating practitioners to take bold steps in their lives. By embracing citrine, witches can channel its energizing qualities to create success and abundance in various facets of their lives.

## *Clear Quartz*

Clear quartz is often referred to as the "master healer" because of its versatility and ability to amplify energy. For cottage witches, clear quartz serves multiple purposes; it can be programmed for specific intentions, used to cleanse other crystals, and facilitate meditation. It's particularly effective in enhancing spiritual work and fostering clarity when communicating with the higher self or spirits. With its pure and potent vibration, clear quartz is an essential tool for amplifying spells, rituals, and intentions, making it invaluable in any witch's toolkit. Many practitioners use clear quartz in crystal grids to magnify the energies of surrounding stones and enhance the overall effectiveness of their magical workings.

In addition to its amplifying properties, clear quartz is also known for its ability to store information and memories. This makes it an excellent choice for use in manifestation rituals, where practitioners can focus their intentions on the stone, allowing it to hold and project their desires into the universe. It excels in energy healing practices as well, aiding in balancing and harmonizing the body's energy systems. Witches often employ clear quartz in rituals to enhance intuition, improve focus, or as a channel for energies during spellcasting. Its adaptability makes it a fundamental crystal for achieving clarity and depth in various aspects of cottage witchcraft.

## *Moonstone*

Moonstone is a mystical stone deeply connected to the energies of the moon and the divine feminine. For cottage witches, moonstone embodies intuition, emotional balance, and transformation. Its ethereal glow resonates with lunar cycles, making it a perfect companion for rituals and spells conducted during the full moon or new moon. Many witches use moonstone to enhance their psychic abilities, increase emotional intelligence, and foster personal growth. Whether it's carried, worn, or placed on an altar, moonstone encourages trust in one's intuition and the cyclical nature of life, thus enhancing a witch's spiritual practice.

In magical practices, moonstone is often associated with journeys of self-discovery and exploration of one's inner depths. Its calming energy can help ease emotional turmoil, making it useful during healing rituals or meditations aimed at nurturing the self. Additionally, moonstone is used for fertility, new beginnings, and protection during travel, particularly at night. Cottage witches may incorporate moonstone into spells for love, intuition, or achieving goals aligned with the moon's phases. The stone's luminescence and mysterious energy make it a cherished asset for any practitioner seeking to embrace the mysteries of the lunar realm.

## *Selenite*

Selenite is a powerful crystal known for its cleansing and purifying properties. For cottage witches, selenite serves as a spiritual tool for clearing stagnant energy and creating a serene environment for magical workings. Its high vibrational frequency can help cleanse and charge other crystals, making it an essential part of any witch's practice. Selenite is often placed in sacred spaces, such as altars or meditation corners, to maintain a clean energy flow and establish a peaceful atmosphere conducive to spiritual growth. Additionally, its connection to the moon enhances rituals focused on intuition and emotional healing.

In spiritual practices, selenite is associated with clarity of thought, spiritual insight, and communication with higher realms. Many witches use selenite wands to channel energy during healing rituals or to set intentions. It can also serve as a tool for grounding and centering, helping practitioners connect with their higher selves and gain insights into their spiritual journeys. Selenite is particularly effective when used during full moons or during meditative practices aimed at gaining clarity. With its ability to foster a strong connection to the etheric realm, selenite stands out as a vital ally for witches seeking to deepen their spiritual and magical practices.

## *Malachite*

Malachite is a striking green stone known for its transformative properties and strong connection to the earth. For cottage witches, malachite embodies abundance, healing, and protection. It is associated with the heart chakra, making it an essential tool for emotional healing and growth. Malachite encourages self-awareness and personal transformation, making it ideal for powerful rituals focused on release and renewal. Witches often use malachite in spells aimed at attracting abundance or fostering positive changes in life circumstances. Due to its ability to absorb negative energies, it's recommended to cleanse malachite regularly to maintain its effectiveness.

In addition to attracting prosperity, malachite is known for its physical healing properties. It's commonly used in healing practices for issues related to the heart, both emotionally and physically. Witches may incorporate malachite into crystal grids focused on health and well-being, or use it in spells intended to promote courage and empowerment. Its rich green color also symbolizes growth and fertility, making it valuable during seasonal celebrations or rituals focused on new beginnings. Malachite encourages witches to embrace and navigate their emotional landscapes, fostering a deeper understanding of themselves and the transformative journey of life.

## *Tiger's Eye*

Tiger's Eye is a striking, banded stone known for its grounding and protective qualities. This versatile crystal is associated with courage, confidence, and strength—qualities that make it particularly appealing to cottage witches. It resonates with the solar plexus chakra, enhancing personal power and determination. Tiger's Eye is especially valuable for spells focusing on success, courage in facing challenges, and achieving personal goals. By carrying or wearing Tiger's Eye during difficult times or important endeavors, practitioners can harness its empowering energy to help navigate obstacles and promote resilience.

In magical practices, Tiger's Eye can also serve as a shield against negative energies and psychic attacks, promoting an aura of protection around the wearer. Its balancing nature helps harmonize emotional and mental states, making it beneficial for witches engaged in shadow work or personal exploration. Incorporating Tiger's Eye into rituals aimed at manifesting goals or attracting prosperity can amplify intentions and improve focus. Whether used in meditation, spellwork, or simply carried as a talisman, Tiger's Eye inspires courage and confidence, empowering witches to take bold steps on their magical journeys.

When selecting your crystals, consider visiting local shops or seeking out natural formations in nearby areas. Trust your intuition; often, the crystals that draw your attention are those that resonate with your energy.

### How to Cleanse, Charge, and Program Crystals

To harness the full potential of your crystals, it's crucial to regularly cleanse, charge, and program them. This process clears any stagnant energies and aligns the stones with your intentions.

## *Cleansing Crystals*

Cleansing removes any energies that may have accumulated over time, ensuring the crystal vibrates at its purest frequency. Here are several methods to cleanse your stones:

1. **Moonlight**: Leave your crystals outside or on a windowsill during a full moon to absorb the lunar energies. This method is particularly effective for emotional and intuitive stones like moonstone and amethyst.
2. **Running Water**: Hold your crystals under running water—preferably natural sources like a river or stream. Be cautious with soft or porous stones, as water can damage them.

3. **Salt Bath**: Dissolve sea salt in a bowl of water and immerse your crystals (not suitable for all stones). Afterward, rinse with fresh water to remove salty residue.
4. **Smudging**: Use sage, sweetgrass, or palo santo to cleanse crystals through smoke. Pass the stone through the smoke while setting your intention for cleansing.
5. **Earth**: Burying crystals in the earth for a day or two allows them to absorb grounding energies and release anything that doesn't serve them.

## *Charging Crystals*

Once cleansed, it's important to charge your crystals to amplify their energy. Here are some methods:

1. **Sunlight**: Place your crystals under the sunlight for a few hours. Be mindful that some stones can fade in direct sunlight, so choose this method carefully.
2. **Crystalline Charging**: Arrange your crystals in a grid with larger clusters (e.g., clear quartz) to enhance their energy.
3. **Sound**: Use sound bowls, tuning forks, or bells to raise the vibrational frequency of your crystals. Gently strike or ring your chosen instrument nearby.

## *Programming Crystals*

Programming your crystal involves setting an intention that aligns with your goals or wishes. Here's how to do it effectively:

1. **Clear Your Mind**: Find a quiet space where you won't be interrupted. Take a few deep breaths to center yourself.
2. **Hold Your Crystal**: Place the stone in the palms of your hands and focus your energy on it. Visualize the intention you wish to set.
3. **Speak Aloud**: Clearly articulate your intention. For example, state, "I program this amethyst to bring clarity and peace into my life."
4. **Repeat and Trust**: Visualize your intention manifesting as you repeat the affirmation several times, trusting that the crystal will help you achieve it.

**Incorporating Crystals into Everyday Life and Home Decor**

Integrating crystals into your daily life can elevate your home's energy and enhance your witchcraft practices. Here are various ways to incorporate these beautiful stone allies into your home:

**1. Jewelry:**

Make or purchase crystal jewelry—like bracelets, pendants, or rings. Wearing crystals close to your body allows you to carry their energies throughout the day.

**2. Altars and Sacred Spaces:**

Create an altar using your chosen crystals, placing them alongside candles, ritual items, and herbs. This sacred space serves as a focal point for your magical practices and intentions.

**3. Home Decor:**

Place crystals in various rooms to enhance their energy. A cluster of amethyst can be both decorative and beneficial in a living room, while a bowl of citrine on the kitchen counter invites abundance during meals.

**4. Meditation Practices:**

Incorporate crystals into your meditation routine. Choose a crystal that aligns with your intention for the session, holding it in your hand or placing it nearby.

**5. Crystal Grids:**

Design a crystal grid for specific intentions using various stones. This can be done in any room and can help manifest desires like love, protection, or prosperity.

**6. Garden Enhancements:**

Consider using crystals in your garden to attract positive energy to your plants. Buried stones can promote growth, while decorative stones can beautify the exterior of your home.

**7. Energy Cleansing Stations:**

Set up small areas throughout your home that include cleansing items like selenite and salt bowls. This encourages ongoing energetic hygiene throughout your living space.

**8. Intention Stones:**

Place crystals with specific intentions in strategic locations —like rose quartz near your bedside for love or black tourmaline in your workspace for protection.

Crystals and gemstones are invaluable companions for the cottage witch, serving as conduits for natural energies and a means to express intention. By selecting, cleansing, charging, and programming crystals, you can deepen your magical practices while inviting beauty and positivity into your life and home.

Whether used to enhance your personal energy or integrated into your space for decor and harmony, crystals can significantly impact your practice. As you explore the world of stones, remember to trust your intuition and enjoy the journey of discovery.

# Chapter 10: Divination Practices

∞∞∞

As a cottage witch, my connection to nature has always played an integral role in my practice. I find solace and wisdom in the natural world around me, and over time, I've come to rely on its offerings for divination. My journey has been one of exploration, intuition, and a deeper understanding of the earth's rhythms.

## The Allure of Nature's Tools

One late afternoon, I was feeling a bit lost and sought guidance. I wandered outside to my garden breathing in the scents of herbs and blossoms. That's when I first noticed how many natural items around me held potential for divination.

## Leaves and Petals

One of my favorite forms of natural divination is leaf reading. I would collect fallen leaves from different trees, each resonating with unique energies. As I spread them out on my table, I'd look for patterns, colors, and even imperfections. Each leaf seemed to tell a story. For example, the vibrant green of a maple leaf would symbolize growth and renewal, while the crinkled edges of an autumn leaf whispered of change and letting go.

Petals, too, became my allies. During the blooming season, I would gather flowers from my garden, grounding myself in their fragrances and colors. By laying out the petals in a circle,

I created a mini altar that reflected my current emotional state. The interpretation was often intuitive – the way the petals landed, their vibrancy, and even the arrangement would guide me toward understanding my inner landscape and the questions I was grappling with.

**Stones and Crystals**

Stones, with their ancient wisdom, also became crucial to my divination practice. I started to collect smooth river stones and crystals during my nature walks. Each stone I chose felt remarkably unique, resonating with specific energies and vibrations. I developed a practice of holding a stone, closing my eyes, and allowing its energy to wash over me while pondering a question.

One day, I sat on the banks of a nearby stream, feeling particularly indecisive about a life change. I picked up a clear quartz crystal, holding it against my heart. As I breathed deeply, I felt a rush of clarity and intuition guiding me toward a path I had been hesitant to embrace. The rock became my talisman, reminding me of that moment of insight whenever I held it.

**Driftwood and Dried Herbs**

Driftwood collected from the river's edge became another tool for my divination. I crafted a simple pendulum using a piece of driftwood and a string made from natural fibers. With this, I would ask questions about my future, allowing the pendulum's swinging to guide my decisions. The gentle sway of nature's creation became a symbol of the flow of life, reminding me to trust my intuition as I navigated my path.

Dried herbs also found their way into my divination toolkit. I often created herbal sachets with specific intentions, using rosemary for clarity, chamomile for peace, and lavender for love. The process of crafting these sachets was meditative, and once complete, I would carry them with me or place them on my altar as an open channel for guidance.

**Embracing Intuition**

Through my exploration with natural items, I've learned that divination is as much about intuition as it is about the tools themselves. Every leaf, stone, and petal seems to resonate with an energy that can be felt when I am in tune with my inner self. Nature provides a vast array of resources, but the most significant aspect is the bond I've formed with the earth and its cycles.

Each experience deepens my understanding of the interconnectedness between myself and the natural world. The whispers of the wind, the rustling of leaves, and the sparkle of dew on grass all become parts of a dialogue that guides me and reflects my inner journey.

As a cottage witch using natural items for divination, I've come to appreciate the beauty of simplicity. There is magic in the world around us, waiting to be unraveled – one leaf, stone, and flower at a time. It's an ongoing journey, one filled with lessons, insights, and a deepening relationship with the earth that I cherish immensely.

## *The Art of Divination*

Divination, the ancient art of seeking knowledge of the future or the unknown, has captivated human imagination for centuries. From the mystical allure of tarot cards to the wisdom of runes and oracle decks, the tools of divination serve as mirrors reflecting our inner thoughts, feelings, and potential paths. Let me go over the various divination tools, provide simple methods for daily guidance, and discuss how to effectively document your readings in your Book of Shadows.

Overview of Various Divination Tools

## *Tarot Cards*

Tarot cards have long been one of the most popular tools for divination. A typical tarot deck comprises 78 cards divided into two main sections: the Major Arcana (22 cards) and the Minor Arcana (56 cards).

- **Major Arcana**: These cards represent significant life events and transformative experiences. They guide individuals through the major themes of life's journey. Each card, such as The Fool or The Tower, has rich symbolism and meaning, often tied to archetypal narratives.

- **Minor Arcana**: The Minor Arcana is further divided into four suits: Cups, Pentacles, Swords, and Wands. Each suit covers different facets of life—emotions, material aspects, intellect, and action, respectively. Each card within these suits can provide nuanced insights into day-to-day matters.

*Uses*: Tarot can be used for various purposes, including self-reflection, problem-solving, or predicting potential outcomes in personal situations. Layouts (or spreads) can range from a simple three-card spread for past, present, and future readings to complex arrangements like the Celtic Cross.

## *Oracle Cards*

Unlike tarot decks, which follow a specific structure, oracle cards can vary significantly in themes and designs. An oracle deck may consist of anywhere from 40 to over 100 cards, often featuring unique illustrations and interpretations related to a chosen theme, such as angels, nature, or affirmations.

*Uses*: Oracle decks provide a more free-flowing approach to divination, allowing for intuitive interpretation. You may select a single card for simple messages or perform more elaborate spreads tailored to personal or spiritual queries. The broad flexibility makes oracle readings accessible to all levels of practitioners.

## *Runes*

Runes originate from ancient Germanic alphabets that were utilized in both writing and divination. A typical rune set comprises 24 symbols (elder futhark) representing various elements of existence, nature, and human experience.

*Uses*: To use runes, practitioners generally cast a handful onto a surface or draw a random rune from a pouch, allowing the symbols to convey messages. Each rune has specific meanings, deeply rooted in mythology and historical context, ranging from guidance and insights to warnings and affirmations.

## *Additional Tools*

Beyond the three popular tools above, several other divination practices include:

- **I Ching**: An ancient Chinese divination text, often used with yarrow sticks or coins to yield hexagrams that relate to life's cyclical nature.
- **Pendulums**: Utilizing the subconscious energy, pendulums can assist in making decisions or seeking answers to specific yes/no questions.
- **Scrying**: The practice of gazing into reflective surfaces, such as crystal balls or water, to perceive visions and

gather intuitive insights.

**Simple Methods for Daily Divination and Intuitive Guidance**

**Daily Tarot Draw**

Start each day by drawing a single tarot card. Take a moment to meditate on the card, reflecting on its meaning and how it might apply to your day ahead. Ask yourself how the card's themes can guide your approach to situations, interactions, or challenges.

**Example**: If you draw The Sun, embrace optimism and positive energy throughout your day. Conversely, if you draw The Devil, consider where you might feel trapped or tempted, and focus on overcoming those hurdles.

**Oracle Card Pull**

Choose an oracle card each morning as a message from your higher self, spirit guides, or the universe. Interpret the card's meaning as it relates to your current circumstances and intentions, allowing its guidance to shape your mindset for the day.

**Example**: Drawing an "Abundance" card may remind you to remain open to opportunities and gratitude, influencing how you approach work and relationships.

**Rune Casting**

For those who wish to incorporate runes into their daily practice, select a rune each day. Cast a handful of runes or draw one from a pouch, and reflect on its meaning in the context of your life.

**Example**: Drawing the rune Wunjo (Joy) can inspire feelings of happiness and connection, while Nautiz (Need) might signal a need for self-care or addressing a particular challenge.

## Recording Readings in Your Book of Shadows

A Book of Shadows serves as a personal journal for your spiritual practice, allowing you to document your divination readings and the insights gained. Here's how to effectively record your divination experiences:

### Organizing Your Entries

1. **Date and Time**: Note when the reading took place for future reference and reflection.
2. **Type of Reading**: Specify which tool you used (tarot, oracle, runes, etc.) and the format of your spread or method.
3. **Card/Rune Selection**: Draw or describe the card(s) or rune(s) used in the reading. Include images when possible.
4. **Interpretation**: Record your initial thoughts and feelings about each card or symbol, including any intuitive insights that arose during the reading.
5. **Context**: Describe your current life situation and any specific questions or concerns you intended to explore during your session.
6. **Reflection**: After some time has passed (days or weeks), return to your entries to reflect on outcomes, unexpected developments, and how the readings influenced your decisions.

### Example Entry

**Date**: October 14, 2023
**Tool**: Tarot
**Spread**: Three-card draw

**Cards**:

- **Past:** Three of Swords (heartbreak and sorrow)
- **Present:** The Empress (creativity and nurturing)
- **Future:** Ace of Pentacles (new opportunities and abundance)

**Interpretation**: The Three of Swords reflects recent emotional pain. Currently, The Empress encourages me to nurture myself and cultivate positivity. The Ace of Pentacles hints that a fruitful opportunity is emerging following a time of struggle.

**Context**: I was feeling overwhelmed by disappointment after a recent breakup and sought clarity on my emotional healing journey.

**Reflection**: A week later, I received an unexpected job offer, illustrating the Ace of Pentacles. Focusing on nurturing myself allowed me to embrace this opportunity.

Incorporating divination practices into your daily routine can deepen self-awareness, enhance intuition, and facilitate personal growth. By understanding various tools and methods, you create a powerful form of self-expression and guidance. As you document your readings, your Book of Shadows transforms into a dynamic record of your spiritual journey, providing an invaluable reference for the growth and wisdom you continue to cultivate.

# Chapter 11: Spirits of the Land

∞∞∞

In the heart of the cottage witchery practice lies a profound connection to the natural world—an intimate bond with the very fabric of life surrounding us. With this in mind, let's acknowledge the rich tapestry of spirits residing in these landscapes, the ancestors who walked before us, and the deep-seated folklore that shapes our understanding of these entities. It is here we discover the essence of honoring the spirits of the land and the unspeakable wisdom embedded within our local ecosystems.

### Connecting with Local Nature Spirits and Ancestors

## *The Nature Spirits*

Nature spirits—often seen as the guardians of the earth—embody the life force of the environment. These entities, which can include elementals such as sprites, fae, dryads, and sylphs, manifest the energy of their respective elements: earth, air, fire, and water. To connect with these beings, a witch must cultivate a relationship that transcends mere observation and fosters genuine communion.

1. **Observational Connection:** Begin by spending time in

nature—whether it's a nearby forest, a riverbank, or your own garden. Pay attention to the subtle signs: the way the wind whispers, the way the trees sway, and the sounds of rustling leaves. Bring a journal to note your observations, feelings, and experiences. This practice not only heightens your awareness of local spirits but also allows you to develop your intuition.

**2. Intentional Offerings and Communication:** Creating dedicated spaces in nature, such as an altar or a specific area adorned with flowers and crystals, can facilitate communication with these spirits. Offerings can range from pieces of bread or fruit to flowers or handmade crafts. When presenting these offerings, speak from the heart, inviting them to join you in your magical practice. Be open to receiving signs, messages, or feelings in response.

**3. Ritual Practices:** Engaging in ritualistic practices can help strengthen your bond with nature spirits. This can include simple invocations during the full moon or seasonal celebrations where you call upon the spirits of the land.

## *Ancestral Connections*

Our ancestors embody the wisdom and experiences of those who came before us. In cottage witchery, one recognizes that their spirits guide and protect us, offering insight derived from generations past.

**1. Genealogy Exploration:** Understanding your lineage is pivotal for connecting with your ancestors. Research your family tree and uncover the stories, cultures, and traditions that shaped your ethnic background. This exploration might lead to deeper connections with particular customs or spiritual practices that resonate with you.

**2. Ancestral Altars:** Constructing an ancestral altar within your home or a specific sacred space can help honor those who have shaped your existence. This altar might hold photographs, heirlooms, or items that represent your lineage, alongside candles and offerings to invite their presence. Regularly visiting this altar to reflect, meditate, or talk to them can foster a deeper connection.

**3. Dreamwork and Meditation:** Invite your ancestors to participate in your dreams or visions through dedicated meditation sessions. Ask them to impart wisdom or guidance and keep a journal of your experiences to help reflect upon and interpret any messages you receive.

## Understanding the Role of Folklore and Mythology in Cottage Witchery

**The Significance of Folklore**

Cottage witchery thrives on the stories that connect us to the natural world. Folklore—rich with wisdom, culture, and morality—bridges the gap between the tangible and the spiritual. These narratives often feature local spirits, reflecting the qualities of the land's elements and the relationship between humans and nature.

**1. Local Legends and Myths:** Dive into the folklore of your area. Research tales and legends passed down through generations, seeking those that resonate with themes of nature spirits or ancestors. These stories enrich your understanding of the local spirits and serve as a foundation for your practices.

**2. Community Storytelling:** Engage with your community by sharing these legends or discovering newer tales. This communal exchange and participation deepen your connection to your ancestors and the spirits, enriching your craft.

3. **Personalization of Folklore:** As a cottage witch, allow your own experiences to inform the stories you tell and live by. Combine traditional folklore with your unique interpretations and insights, creating a personal narrative that centers your practice.

**Myths and Archetypes**

Many nature spirits embody archetypes derived from mythology. Understanding these archetypes can provide significant insight into their roles and characteristics, informing your magical workings.

1. **The Earth Mother:** Often depicted in various cultures as the nurturing aspect of nature, the Earth Mother represents fertility, growth, and abundance. Cultivating a relationship with her archetype can inspire rituals centered on gratitude and prosperity.

2. **The Trickster:** Trickster spirits in folklore embody the spirit of mischief and balance. They challenge established norms and encourage flexibility in thinking. When faced with challenges, connecting with trickster energies can help you embrace change and adaptability.

3. **The Protectors:** Many folklore traditions speak of spirits or deities protecting specific landscapes or natural features. Honor these protectors through gratitude rituals that acknowledge their guardianship over the land and its resources.

**Rituals for Honoring Spirits of the Land**

**Seasonal Festivals**

Each season offers unique opportunities to honor the spirits that resonate with natural cycles. Celebrating these transformations can create a powerful connection to both nature and local spirits.

1. **Spring Renewal Ritual:** As life begins to bloom, celebrate the rebirth experienced in nature. Prepare a simple gathering outdoors with flowers, seeds, and herbal teas. Invite the spirits of growth and renewal to join you as you plant seeds, sharing your intentions for what you wish to cultivate in the forthcoming season.

2. **Autumn Harvest Ritual:** Before winter wraps its arms around the earth, hold a harvest celebration, thanking the spirits for the abundance of the year. Create an altar filled with seasonal produce and partake in a feast with friends, uplifting the energy of gratitude and connection.

## Ancestral Ceremony

Once a year, dedicate a special day to honor your ancestors by performing a ceremony that bridges the past with the present.

1. **Preparation:** Gather artifacts that resonate with you, such as photos, recipes, or items belonging to family members. Create a sacred space—free from disturbances—where you can invoke their energy and presence.

2. **Invocation:** Begin with a moment of silence. Light candles and call upon each ancestor by name, sharing stories and memories that evoke gratitude and love. This can include sharing a meal made from family recipes or engaging in activities that remind you of them.

## Elemental Offerings

Incorporating elements into your rituals allows for an innate connection to the spirit world.

> **1. Earth:** Create a small mound of soil and dedicate it to the earth spirits, visualizing your intentions and sealing them within the ground. Alternatively, bury small tokens during your offerings at the foot of a tree.
>
> **2. Water:** Visit a body of water and recite a prayer of thanks, casting flower petals, stones, or herbs as offerings. Allow the currents to carry your intentions to the spirits that dwell within the water.
>
> **3. Fire:** Construct a small bonfire or use candles to represent the spirit of fire. Burning herbs like sage or incense during your rituals can offer transformation and clearing, inviting fire spirits to join you.

As we embark on connecting with the spirits of the land, we celebrate both the visible and invisible forces that shape our experience. The wisdom of our ancestors, the energy of nature spirits, and the stories that bind us to our environment all contribute to a holistic witchcraft practice. I hope to inspire you to nurture your relationship with the land and honor the spirits that dwell in the heart of your ancestry.

# Chapter 12: Candle Magic & Spellcrafting

∞∞∞

Candle magic is an ancient practice that has stood the test of time, utilized by many spiritual traditions to channel energy, set intentions, and invoke results. You should become familiar with the basics of candle magic, the process of creating and casting your spells, and essential safety tips and ethical considerations for effective spellwork.

## Basics of Candle Magic

**Colors**

Candle colors play an essential role in focusing energy and enhancing your intentions. Different colors represent different aspects of life and correspond to specific intentions:

- **White**: Purity, protection, and healing. Can be used for any purpose.
- **Black**: Banishing negativity, protection, and grounding. Useful for reversing curses or eliminating unwanted influences.
- **Red**: Passion, strength, and love. Suitable for matters of the heart, courage, and vitality.

- **Pink**: Compassion, romance, and friendship. Ideal for love and emotional healing situations.
- **Green**: Prosperity, growth, and abundance. Used for financial success, fertility, and new beginnings.
- **Blue**: Peace, tranquility, and communication. Great for soothing emotions and improving communication.
- **Yellow**: Clarity, creativity, and intellect. Effective for mental growth, concentration, and boosting confidence.
- **Purple**: Spiritual awareness, intuition, and power. Associated with higher wisdom and connections to the divine.
- **Orange**: Creativity, enthusiasm, and change. Good for motivation and stimulating new ideas.
- **Gold**: is linked to wealth, success, and solar energy, embodying confidence and illumination in magical workings.
- **Silver**: represents intuition, emotional balance, and lunar energies, fostering deep connections and spiritual insights in magical endeavors.

When selecting your candle color, ensure that it resonates with your specific goal to amplify your magical working.

**Shapes**

Candles come in various shapes, each imparting distinct energies and purposes:

- **Pillar Candles**: Versatile and commonly used in spellwork, they represent stability and strength.
- **Taper Candles**: For rituals requiring energy flow; they can be placed on altars for directional energy.

- **Jar Candles**: Contained in glass; useful for long-term workings and can hold additional herbs or oils.
- **Votive Candles**: Short-term use and excellent for focused spells. Easy to place in small spaces or altars.
- **Figure Candles**: Represent specific individuals or concepts; used for personal work or to symbolize someone in your spell.

Choose the candle shape that best fits the occasion and the specific intention of your spell.

**Intentions**

At the heart of candle magic lies intention. Intentions should be clear, focused, and positively phrased. When crafting spells, particularly those that may influence others, their importance cannot be understated. The clarity of your intention sets the stage for successful manifestation. To enhance this focus:

- Write down your intention clearly. This can serve as a focal point throughout your working.
- Visualize your desired outcome as you prepare to light the candle.
- Speak your intention aloud, infusing it with your energy.

## *Creating and Casting Your Own Spells*

### *Step 1: Preparation*

- **Gather Supplies**: Candles, herbs, oils, a fireproof dish, and anything else that resonates with your intention, such as crystals or personal items.

- **Create Sacred Space**: Designate a quiet area for your work. Cleanse the space using sage, salt, or through visualization.

## *Step 2: Anointing and Dressing Candles*

Before using a candle, it's common practice to dress it with oils and herbs related to your intention. Olive oil is a popular base oil, but you can use others according to your preference.

1. **Anoint the Candle**: Begin at the middle of the candle and move upward, then downward to bring energy both into the candle and back out into the world.
2. **Add Herbs**: Roll the candle in herbs associated with your intention. For example, if you're working on attracting love, you might use basil or rose petals.

## *Step 3: Casting the Spell*

1. **Set the Intention**: Hold the candle in your hands and visualize your intention clearly, feeling the energy surging through you and into the candle.
2. **Light the Candle**: As you ignite the wick, state your intention out loud, signaling to the universe that you are ready to manifest your desires.
3. **Focus**: Spend a few moments meditating, visualizing your intention and allowing energy to flow towards it. You might even chant a mantra or incantation to further solidify your connection.

## Step 4: Closing

Once you feel your energy has been fully channeled into the spell, close it by thanking the energies you have invoked—this could include deities, spirits, or simply the universe itself. Allow the candle to burn out completely unless you're using it for a multi-day spell, in which case snuff it out respectfully, never blowing it out, as it can scatter the energy of your intention.

**Safety Tips**

1. **Fire Safety**: Always supervise candles while lit, and ensure they are in a sturdy holder away from flammable objects.
2. **Ventilation**: Make sure the area is well-ventilated, especially if using scented candles or incense.
3. **Disposal**: When the candle is finished, dispose of the remains ethically—burial is often recommended to release the energies safely into the earth.

**Ethical Considerations for Spellwork**

Candle magic, though powerful, carries a profound responsibility. Practitioners must consider the ethical implications of their work:

1. **Free Will**: Respect the free will of others. While you may wish to attract love or success, focus on your own characteristics or circumstances rather than attempting to manipulate someone else's feelings or actions.
2. **Positive Intentions**: Always aim to manifest with positive intentions. Spells designed to harm or manipulate can lead to karmic repercussions. Strive for

outcomes that benefit not just yourself but others in the wider community.

3. **Accountability**: Be prepared for the consequences of your spellwork, whether it leads to success or failure. Understand that energy spent in the process may return to you in unexpected ways.

Candle magic is a potent tool for spiritual practitioners, offering individuals a path to focus their intentions and manifest their desires. By understanding the essentials of color, shape, and intention while adhering to ethical guidelines and safety tips, one can engage in candle magic effectively and responsibly.

With practice, you can develop a profound and transformative relationship with this art, harnessing its power for your highest good and the betterment of all. This art of spellcrafting, when approached thoughtfully and with respect, can open doors to possibilities and personal growth that exceed your desires.

# Chapter 13: Intention & Visualization

∞∞∞

In the realm of magical practices, the power of intention and visualization serves as one of the foundational pillars upon which success is built. Intentions are like the seeds we plant in the fertile ground of our consciousness, while visualization acts as the sunlight and water, nurturing those seeds into fruition. Let's illuminate how you can harness these powers to enhance your magical practice, explore effective techniques for visualization and manifestation, and share insights on journaling for reflection and growth.

**Setting Intentions for Your Magical Practice**

Setting intentions is an essential step that delineates the purpose behind every magical act. It infuses your practice with clarity and direction, allowing your energy to align with the desired outcome. But what does it mean to set an intention, and how can one do it effectively?

1. **Understanding Intentions**: Intentions are not just wishes or vague hopes; they are clear, focused statements that articulate what you want to achieve. An intention should resonate with your true self and align with your values, for only then can it catalyze genuine transformation.
2. **Crafting Your Intention**:

- **Be Specific**: Rather than saying, "*I want to be happy,*" an intention might be, "*I intend to cultivate joy by embracing self-love and gratitude in my daily life.*"
- **Use Positive Language**: Frame your intention in affirmative terms. Instead of, "*I do not want to feel anxious,*" try, "*I intend to feel calm and centered in all situations.*"
- **Make It Timeless**: Your intention should feel relevant irrespective of the time frame. Rather than tying it to a specific date, affirm it as a constant aspect of your life.

3. **Ritualize Your Intentions**: Highlight the importance of creating a ceremony or ritual that embodies your intention. This could be the lighting of a candle, creating a sigil, or invoking deities. Celebrate the act of declaring your intention, as it reinforces your commitment.
4. **Daily Affirmation**: Revisit your intention regularly. This can be through daily affirmations, meditations, or mantras that keep your goal alive in your consciousness.

**Techniques for Visualization and Manifestation**

Visualization is a powerful tool that enables you to vividly imagine your intentions as present realities. It is through the act of seeing in your mind's eye that you can convince your subconscious to act in accordance with your desires. Here are some techniques to enhance your visualization and manifestation skills:

1. **Meditative Visualization**:
    - Find a quiet space, close your eyes, and take several deep breaths. Allow your body to relax.

- Visualize a warm, radiant light surrounding you, representing your intention. Imagine this light growing stronger, filling you with its energy.
- Picture the desired outcome: see yourself interacting with it. If your intention is love, visualize sharing joyful moments with your partner, feeling loved and cherished.

2. **Vision Boards:**
   - Collect images, words, and symbols that resonate with your intention. A vision board visually anchors your desires, acting as a constant reminder of what you seek to manifest.
   - Arrange these items on a board, in a space you frequently engage with. Spend a few minutes each day gazing at it, allowing yourself to feel the emotions associated with achieving those desires.

3. **Scripting:**
   - Write a narrative as if your intention has already been fulfilled. Describe your life, feelings, and actions in vivid detail. This process helps solidify the energy behind your intentions.
   - Read your script daily, allowing yourself to fully experience the emotions tied to that narrative.

4. **The 'Feeling' Technique:**
   - Visualize the end result of your intention and focus on the emotions you would experience once it's realized. Cultivate those feelings in the present moment, charging your intention with genuine emotion—the emotional component amplifies the manifestation process.

**Journaling for Reflection and Growth**

Journaling is an invaluable tool in the magical practitioner's arsenal. It facilitates deep reflection, providing a space to articulate thoughts and experiences, track progress, and foster personal growth. Here's how to integrate journaling into your magical practice:

1. **Intentional Journaling**:
   - Begin each journaling session by revisiting your intentions. Write them down and explore new ways to integrate them into your life.
   - Reflect on how your actions align with your intentions. Where have you succeeded? Where could you improve?

2. **Daily Reflection**:
   - At the end of each day, jot down moments when you felt aligned with your intention. What actions did you take? What emotions did you experience?
   - Conversely, write about any challenges you faced. Recognize patterns that may reveal limiting beliefs or unconscious blocks.

3. **Gratitude Entries**:
   - Reinforce positivity by maintaining a section for gratitude. Acknowledging what you appreciate in your life amplifies your energy and aligns with the law of attraction.
   - Aim to write at least three things you are grateful for daily, reinforcing the abundance mindset.

4. **Dream and Intuition Logs**:
   - Keep track of your dreams and any intuitive nudges. Often, these can reveal insights about your intentions or guide your next steps in your practice.
   - Date your entries and reflect on their relevance to

your current journey.

The power of intention and visualization are invaluable assets in your magical practice, shaping the way you interact with the energies of the universe. By setting clear intentions, engaging in effective visualization techniques, and reflective journaling, you develop a focused practice that not only manifests desires but also nurtures personal growth.

As you amplify your consciousness, you align more deeply with your authentic self, ultimately harnessing the mystical forces around you to create a life imbued with purpose and fulfillment. I hope these concepts continue to guide and inspire you as you embark on your journey of discovery and empowerment through magic.

# Chapter 14: Community & Collaboration

∞∞∞

In the intricate tapestry of witchcraft, the power of community and collaboration emerges as a vital thread, weaving individual practitioners into a collective force that enhances both personal practice and the broader goals of witchcraft. I want to review the significance of building a supportive witch community, engaging in collaborative rituals and gatherings, and sharing knowledge, resources, and tools. Through this exploration, we will uncover the many facets of community that enrich the lives of witches and empower their craft.

**Building a Supportive Witch Community**

At the heart of any thriving witch community lies support —an essential ingredient that cultivates a sense of belonging and fosters growth. Building a supportive witch community requires intention, openness, and a mutual commitment to uplift one another. There are several steps to establishing and nurturing this environment.

**1. Intentional Networking**

To build a community, begin by identifying your goals. Are you seeking like-minded individuals for friendship, collaboration on rituals, or a resource for learning? Once your intentions are clear, utilize social media platforms, local notice boards, and spiritual shops to connect with others. Online forums, Facebook groups, and local meet-ups can foster friendships that span geographical boundaries.

## 2. Inclusivity and Respect

A successful witch community thrives on inclusivity. Acknowledge and celebrate the diverse paths within witchcraft. Everyone's journey is unique, whether they practice Wicca, traditional witchcraft, hedge witchery, or another form of the Craft. Respect differing beliefs and practices, foster an environment where discussions ignite inspiration, and create room for individuals to express who they are without fear of judgment.

## 3. Creating a Safe Space

Safety—both physical and emotional—is crucial in building community. Establish clear boundaries and guidelines for gatherings; these can range from respecting privacy to encouraging open dialogue. Create a welcoming atmosphere where members feel free to share their experiences, struggles, and triumphs without fear of stigma or disapproval. This can be achieved through regular check-ins and establishing member guidelines that promote kindness and respect.

## Collaborative Rituals and Gatherings

Once a community foundation has been established, the next step involves creating communal experiences through collaborative rituals and gatherings. These shared moments amplify individual energies, creating a collective force that can be both potent and transformative.

## 1. Crafting Collaborative Rituals

Collaborative rituals can take various forms, from seasonal celebrations to moon ceremonies or healing rituals for community members in need. Here's how to approach them:

- **Identify a Purpose**: Closing of a season, a particular phase of the moon, or a shared goal—what binds the community together? Defining a ritual's purpose ensures that all participants are united in intention.
- **Gather Input**: Invite ideas from all participants. Each member brings unique skills and talents, such as herbal knowledge, musical abilities, or artistic flair. Incorporate these gifts into the ritual design, fostering a sense of contribution and belonging.
- **Assign Roles**: Divide responsibilities openly to ensure everyone feels involved. Assign roles such as ritual leader, altar creator, or song singer. Having a clear structure helps everyone engage meaningfully and enhances the group energy.
- **Choose a Sacred Space**: Whether it's a member's home, a local park, or an intended magical site, be mindful of the setting. Create an environment conducive to spiritual work, with the necessary tools and elements for your ritual.

## 2. Hosting Gatherings

Regular gatherings build camaraderie and deepen connections within the community. These can be casual meet-ups over tea or more structured events focused on learning. Hosting gatherings benefits both the community and individual members.

- **Workshops and Teachings**: Offer spaces for local witches to teach each other. Focus on various subjects such as crystal healing, potion-making, or divination techniques. Create a roster of topics and let members volunteer to lead sessions.

- **Study Groups**: Form study groups for deeper explorations of specific texts, traditions, or practices. This exchange of knowledge fosters learning and appreciation for varied paths within the Craft.
- **Seasonal Celebrations**: Celebrate the Wheel of the Year together. Organize events for Sabbats and Esbats that honor the cycles of nature and bring all members into the collective energy of the season.

**Sharing Knowledge, Resources, and Tools**

The final thread weaving community together is the sharing of knowledge, resources, and tools. The act of sharing not only bolsters individual practices but also strengthens the collective capabilities of the group.

**1. Libraries of Knowledge**

Establish a communal library filled with books on witchcraft, herbalism, astrology, and more. Encourage lending programs where members can take turns using various resources. Furthermore, create a digital repository of articles, videos, and guides accessible to all community members.

**2. Tool Exchange Programs**

Craft tools, herbs, and supplies can often be expensive, especially for those starting their journey. Organize tool exchanges where members can share or trade items like crystals, cauldrons, candles, or magical herbs. Consider creating collective purchasing agreements for frequently used supplies to cultivate an economy of sharing.

**3. Mentorship Programs**

Create mentorship programs within the community that connect seasoned practitioners with beginners. This cultivation of relationships fosters personal growth while ensuring the transfer of knowledge from one generation of witches to the next. Mentorship can involve one-on-one meetings, group teachings, or paired rituals.

**4. Support Circles**

Host regular support circles where members can discuss their journeys, share experiences, and seek guidance. Invite open discussions about personal struggles, successes, and dreams related to their magical practices. These circles emphasize emotional connection and understanding, reinforcing the bond within the community.

The power of community within witchcraft cannot be overstated. By building supportive networks, engaging in collaborative rituals and gatherings, and sharing knowledge and resources, witches strengthen not only their individual practices but also the entire fabric of their craft.

The act of coming together under one shared purpose nurtures our collective growth and fosters a vibrant tapestry of magical practices, shared experiences, and mutual empowerment. In embracing the spirit of community and collaboration, witches can create a thriving ecosystem where magic flourishes, and each individual path is enriched through the shared journey.

# Chapter 15: Animal Guides & Familiar Spirits

∞∞∞

Throughout history, many cultures have recognized the significance of animal guides and familiar spirits in spiritual practices and personal journeys. In witchcraft, these beings hold unique positions, serving not only as allies but also as teachers and protectors. There are multifaceted roles that animal guides and familiars play in witchcraft, how to connect with them, and the importance of providing a safe and supportive environment for our animal companions.

**Understanding the Role of Animal Guides in Witchcraft**

Animal guides, often thought of as spirits or totems, embody specific traits, virtues, and energies that can aid practitioners on their spiritual paths. They offer unique insights and wisdom, reflecting traits that we might need to cultivate within ourselves. Traditionally, different animals are associated with various elements, emotions, and personal characteristics, making them powerful symbols in witchcraft.

1. **Symbolism and Archetypes**: Each animal resonates with different attributes. For example, a lion represents courage and leadership, while a butterfly signifies transformation and rebirth. In witchcraft,

understanding these associations allows practitioners to harness the energy of these animals effectively.

2. **Intuition and Instinct**: Animal guides can enhance our intuition and primal instincts. They often show up in moments of need, guiding us through challenging situations. Being receptive to their messages can deepen our understanding of our inner selves and external circumstances.

3. **Protection and Support**: Many witches view their animal guides as protective spirits. During rituals or times of need, calling upon these guides can offer comfort and strength. They create a buffer against negative energies and emotional turmoil.

4. **Connection with Nature**: Having a relationship with animal guides encourages a profound connection to the natural world. As witches, fostering this bond keeps us grounded and in tune with the cycles of life.

**How to Find and Honor Your Familiar**

Unlike animal guides, familiars are specific animals that often form a close bond with the practitioner, providing companionship and supportive energy. Finding and honoring a familiar involves intended effort, patience, and respect.

1. **Identifying Your Familiar**:
    - **Observation**: Pay attention to animals that consistently appear in your life. This could be through encounters in nature, dreams, or even imagery in art and literature.
    - **Meditation**: Engage in meditative practices focused on connecting with the animal world. Visualization techniques where you imagine yourself in a natural setting may help in discovering a familiar who

resonates with you.

- **Dream Work**: Keep a dream journal and note any recurring symbols or animals. Often, familiars will introduce themselves during dreams, providing symbolic messages or guidance.

2. **Facilitating the Bond**:

- **Respecting Boundaries**: If you find an animal you resonate with, approach it with respect. Observe its behavior and try to understand its needs and preferences. A bond built on mutual respect and understanding is key.

- **Creating Rituals**: Perform intentional rituals to honor your familiar's presence. Light a candle, offer food, or create a small altar space for the animal. This act acknowledges the spirit of the animal and strengthens your connection.

3. **Communicating with Your Familiar**:

- Animals have their unique ways of communicating; learn to read their body language and vocalizations. Spend quality time with your familiar, observing and attuning yourself to its energy.

- Consider using divination tools, such as tarot cards, to ask questions about your relationship with your familiar and how best to nurture it.

**Creating a Safe and Welcoming Space for Animal Companions**

Whether your companion is a familiar spirit or an actual animal, creating a nurturing environment fosters a deeper connection with them.

1. **Physical Space:**
   - **Environment:** Ensure that the space where you interact with your familiar is free from clutter and distractions. Incorporate elements that reflect the natural world, such as plants, crystals, or natural wood.
   - **Safety:** If you have live animals as companions, ensure they have enough space, warmth, and comfort. Designate areas for play and rest, ensuring they feel secure.
2. **Energetic Space:**
   - **Cleansing:** Regularly cleanse your space of negative energies. This can be done through smudging, sound tools, or visualization methods. A clear space fosters a safe environment for both you and your companion.
   - **Crystals and Herbs:** Certain crystals, such as amethyst or black tourmaline, can enhance the energy of your space, making them feel more protective. Likewise, burning herbs associated with peace, such as lavender or sage, can create a calming atmosphere.
3. **Rituals and Practices:**
   - **Daily Rituals:** Incorporate daily rituals that honor your familiar. This could include a dedicated time for meditation, play, or simply being quiet together.
   - **Gratitude and Offerings:** Regularly express gratitude to your companion. This could involve quiet reflection on their presence in your life or offering special treats, regardless of whether they are an animal or a spirit.

Understanding and nurturing the relationship with animal guides and familiar spirits is a critical aspect of witchcraft. These beings provide wisdom, protection, and companionship, enriching our spiritual journeys.

By honoring and creating safe spaces for our companions, we foster bonds that reflect the profound connections humans have shared with the animal world for millennia. In doing so, we not only enhance our magical practices but also reconnect with the natural rhythms of life that sustain us.

# Chapter 16: Crafting Magical Tools

∞∞∞

The art of crafting magical tools is as ancient as the practice of magic itself. Whether wielding a wand for precision, a staff for strength, or creating an altar for focused intention, these tools serve as extensions of our will and energy. There are different types of magical tools you can create, the importance of infusing them with your personal energy and intention, and how to maintain and care for them so they serve you well throughout your magical journey.

### *Witchy Tools*

Below is a list of some common witchcraft tools along with their meanings and uses:

## Altar

- **Meaning/Use**: A designated space for performing rituals and spells, often adorned with candles, crystals, and other tools. It represents the sacred and serves as a focal point for energy.

## Athame

- **Meaning/Use**: A double-edged dagger, often used for directing energy, casting circles, and ceremonial purposes. It represents the element of fire and is often associated with the masculine aspect.

## Bell

- **Meaning/Use:** Used to signify the start or end of a ritual, clear negative energy, or attract spirits. The sound of the bell is thought to break the veil between worlds.

## Besom (Broom)

- **Meaning/Use:** The besom, often referred to simply as a broom, holds significant symbolic and practical importance in witchcraft. Traditionally, it represents cleansing, protection, and the ability to sweep away negative energy or unwanted influences.

## Boline

- **Meaning/Use:** A white-handled knife used for cutting herbs, carving symbols, or making magical tools. It is associated with the element of earth and often serves practical and ceremonial purposes.

## Candles

- **Meaning/Use:** Used in rituals for focus, representation of elements, and visualization. The color of the candle often corresponds to the intention of the spell (e.g., green for prosperity, red for passion).

## Cauldron

- **Meaning/Use**: A symbolic vessel representing transformation, the womb of the goddess, and the element of water. Used for brewing potions, scrying, or as a focal point during rituals.

## Chalice (Cup)

- **Meaning/Use**: A vessel used to hold liquids, often representing the element of water and the feminine aspect. It is used during rituals involving blessings, offerings, or celebratory drinks.

## Crystal Ball

- **Meaning/Use**: A sphere used for scrying or divination to gain insight into the future or uncover hidden truths. It symbolizes clarity and intuition.

## Crystals And Stones

- **Meaning/Use**: Used for their metaphysical properties, different crystals and stones can enhance intentions, protection, healing, or manifestation depending on their attributes.

## Herbs

- **Meaning/Use**: Used in spells, potions, and rituals for their symbolic properties. Each herb has specific meanings and uses such as protection, love, or healing.

## Incense

- **Meaning/Use**: Used to purify the space, enhance meditation, or invoke specific energies or deities.

Different scents correspond to various properties such as protection, love, or healing.

## Pentacle

- **Meaning/Use**: A flat, circular object that is inscribed with a pentagram, representing the element of earth. It is used in rituals for protection, as an altar tool, or as a focus for energy.

## Runes

- **Meaning/Use**: Symbols derived from ancient alphabets, used for divination and spellwork. Runes can evoke specific energies or intentions based on their meanings.

## Spirit Board (Ouija Board)

- **Meaning/Use**: A tool for communicating with spirits. Practitioners use it to ask questions and receive answers through a planchette that moves across the board.

## Tarot Cards

- **Meaning/Use**: A deck of cards used for divination, introspection, and gaining insight into situations. Each card holds specific meanings and symbolism.

## Wand

- **Meaning/Use**: A tool for directing energy, performing spells, and invoking spirits. Typically made of wood or other materials, wands represent the element of air and can embody the personal energy of the witch.

These tools are not mandatory for witchcraft practices; rather, they can serve as aids in focusing energy and intention. Many practitioners adapt or create their tools based on personal significance and preference.

### *DIY Magical Tools*

## Altars

Altars serve as sacred spaces where magic manifests. They can be tailored to fit individual practices.

**Materials Required:**
- A sturdy base (wood, stone, or fabric).
- Ritual items (candles, crystals, pictures, etc.).
- Personal items that resonate with you.

**Setting Up the Altar:**
1. **Choosing a Location**: Find a space that feels sacred and comfortable. Consider both ease of access and the energy of the area.
2. **Constructing the Base**: If you're building your altar from scratch, decide on the dimensions. A small tabletop or a space on a shelf can serve perfectly.
3. **Arranging the Items**: Place items that represent the elements, deities, or intentions you wish to honor. Arrange them thoughtfully and meaningfully while paying attention to the energy flow.
4. **Cleansing and Empowering**: Smudge or cleanse the altar using incense or water. Bless it with your chosen

intent, stating its purpose aloud.

**Infusing Tools with Personal Energy and Intention**

Infusing your tools with personal energy is not only about physical creation but also about energetic connection. When it comes to magical tools, intent is paramount. The energy you imbue in each tool transforms it from an object into a conduit for your personal power.

1. **Connecting with Your Tool**: Spend time in meditation with your crafted tool. Allow yourself to feel its energy and the potential it holds. This can be a silent contemplation or an active visualization.
2. **Rituals of Empowerment**: Incorporate rituals that resonate with your personal practice. You might choose to perform a specific incantation, light a candle while holding the tool, or place it under the moonlight to absorb lunar energy.
3. **Setting Clear Intent**: Clearly define the purpose of your tool. Write down an affirmation or incantation that encapsulates its intent and repeat it while focusing on the connection between you and your tool.

# Besom

**Materials Required:**

**Broomstick (Handle)**

- A sturdy wooden stick (around 4-5 feet long) or a long, straight branch (e.g., birch, hazel, or bamboo).

**Broom Corn or Straw**

- You can use broom corn, dried grasses, or long straw.

Look for materials like:

- Sorghum (broom corn)
- Wheat or rye straw
- Palm fronds

**Binding Material**

- Strong twine or natural twine (e.g., jute or hemp).
- You can also use wire, but natural twine is more traditional.

**Scissors or Pruning Shears**

- For cutting the broom corn or straw to the desired length.

**Knife (optional)**

- For trimming the broomstick or shaping the broom corn.

**Screwdriver (optional)**

- If you want to create a hole in the broomstick to secure the binding.

**Instructions:**

1. **Prepare the Broomstick:**
   - Choose your broomstick and cut it to your desired height (generally between 4 and 5 feet).
   - If desired, carve a small notch near one end of the stick to help secure the binding later.

2. **Gather the Broom Corn or Straw:**
   - Collect enough broom corn or straw to make a head for your besom. You will need a bundle that is at least 12 to 16 inches long and as wide as you want the broom head to be.
   - If using straw, ensure it is dry and clean.

3. **Create the Broom Head:**
   - Lay your broom corn or straw flat on a clean work surface.
   - Arrange the broom corn or straw so that it tapers from the middle to either side, creating a rounded shape.
4. **Secure the Broom Head:**
   - Place the broomstick in the center of the broom corn or straw bundle.
   - Use the binding material to tightly wrap the broom head around the broomstick. Start wrapping about 4-6 inches above the base of the broom head.
   - Make several tight loops to hold the broom corn or straw in place, ensuring it's secure but not too tight to split the materials.
5. **Finish Securing:**
   - Tie off the binding material with a strong knot. You can also create a few cross-wraps to add extra security.
   - If you have used a screwdriver to create a notch, you can tuck the end of the binding into this notch for extra stability.
6. **Trim the Broom Head:**
   - Use scissors or pruning shears to trim the ends of the broom corn or straw to the desired length, making sure it's even.
7. **Optional Decoration:**
   - You can decorate the handle with additional twine, ribbons, or other natural materials for aesthetic appeal.
8. **Final Touches:**

- Inspect your besom to ensure the broom head is firm and secure. Make any final adjustments as needed.

**Usage**

Your besom is now ready for use! In traditional contexts, besoms are often used for sweeping and cleansing spaces, but they can also serve as a decorative piece or a tool in various rituals and ceremonies.

## Staffs

**Materials Required:**

- A longer, thicker branch or a bamboo pole.
- Slicing tool (for carving).
- Optional adornments like beads, feathers, or gemstones.

**Creating the Staff:**

1. **Finding Your Staff**: Choose a piece that feels heavy and grounded. Like wands, staffs also hold specific energies based on their wood type.
2. **Shaping and Carving**:
    - Strip away bark and create an ergonomic grip toward one end.
    - Carve symbols or runes along the length of the staff that are relevant to your intent.
3. **Infusing and Personalizing**:
    - You can perform a similar energy infusion with your staff as with wands. Add your personal touch by attaching mementos that hold significant meaning for you, creating a direct link between you and your tool.

# Wands

**Materials Required:**

- A sturdy, straight branch (consider using woods like willow, oak, or cherry for their magical correspondences).
- A small knife or cutting tool (for shaping).
- Sandpaper (for smoothing).
- Optional: Crystals, metals, or natural decoration (to embellish).

**Instructions:**

1. **Selecting the Wood:** The selection of your wand's core wood is pivotal. Each type of wood carries its own magical properties. For instance, cedar enhances protection, while rosewood promotes love and compassion.
2. **Shaping the Wand:**
   - Start by cutting the branch to your desired length, typically between 10 to 15 inches.
   - Use your knife to taper one end, creating a point. This is the end from which you will channel energy.
   - Once shaped, use sandpaper for a smooth finish, removing any rough edges.
3. **Infusing with Intent:**
   - Hold the wand in both hands and close your eyes. Visualize the energy from your body flowing into it.
   - Speak words of empowerment, stating your intent for the wand (e.g., "This wand is a vessel of my will and creativity.").
4. **Decoration:** If you wish to enhance your wand, you

can wrap it with natural fibers, attach crystals with wire, or even carve symbols into it that resonate with your purpose.

## *Maintenance and Care for Your Magical Tools*

Just as a physical tool needs care for optimal performance, magical tools require maintenance to retain their efficacy and connection to your energy.

**Regular Cleansing**

- **Smoke Cleansing**: Use sage, incense, or any preferred herb to smoke cleanse your tools regularly, helping to release stagnant energy.
- **Water Cleansing**: For tools that are water-safe (e.g., wood and crystal), submerge them briefly or sprinkle them with water, picturing the water as a purifier.

**Energy Recharging**

- **Earth Charging**: Burying your wand or staff in the ground for a short period allows it to reconnect with earthy energies.
- **Sun and Moon Charging**: Expose your tools to direct sunlight or moonlight, allowing them to absorb these celestial energies. Full moons are especially potent for recharging.

**Storage**

- **Dedicated Space**: Store your tools in a designated safe spot, such as a cloth bag or a wooden box, to prevent any negative energies from affecting them.
- **Respect and Reverence**: Treat your tools with respect; abstain from using them for trivial purposes. This reinforces their sacred role in your practice.

**Periodic Check-ins**

Regularly check in with your magical tools; observe if they feel "off" or diminished in power. This can guide you in recharging or reinfusing them as required. Develop a routine where you take each tool into your hand and evaluate how it resonates.

Crafting magical tools is a deeply personal and empowering process that bridges the tangible and the ethereal. By understanding the materials, infusing them with your intent, and providing proper care and maintenance, you can create instruments that not only serve your magical practice but also enhance your connection to the mysteries of the universe.

Each wand, staff, and altar becomes an ally on your journey, harmonizing your energy with the forces of creation. Embrace the artistry involved in this sacred craft, and let your tools guide you towards your desired reality.

# Chapter 17: Deities & Archetypes

∞∞∞

The practice of engaging with deities and archetypes can transform your spiritual journey, providing depth, guidance, and a powerful connection to the divine tapestry of existence. Let's review how you can find the right deities and archetypes for your personal practice, build meaningful relationships with these divine energies, and engage in rituals to honor and invoke their presence.

**Finding the Right Deities or Archetypes for Your Practice**

## Understanding Deities and Archetypes

Deities are often understood as divine beings that embody specific qualities or powers within various spiritual traditions. Archetypes, on the other hand, are universal symbols and themes that manifest in our lives and the collective unconscious, as described by the psychologist Carl Jung. They represent fundamental human experiences and emotions, offering ways to access deeper aspects of ourselves and the world around us.

**Self-Reflection and Intuition**

The journey to finding the right deities or archetypes begins with self-reflection. Consider your personal values, experiences, and aspirations. What resonates deeply with you? Are there specific qualities you wish to cultivate, such as strength, wisdom, love, or creativity? Keep a journal to explore these inner landscapes and note any recurring themes or symbols that arise.

**Cultural Connections**

If you're drawn to specific cultures or mythologies, research their pantheons and archetypes, seeking those that resonate with your journey. For instance, if you feel a connection to the natural world, deities associated with nature, Earth, or the cycles of life may be particularly meaningful. Remember to approach this practice with respect and an understanding of the cultural and historical contexts of these deities.

**Signs and Synchronicity**

Pay attention to signs and synchronicities in your life. You might encounter particular symbols, animals, or words that keep appearing, suggesting a connection with certain energies. This might be a favorite flower, an animal that keeps showing up, or a recurring theme in your dreams. Trust your intuition, as these signs may guide you toward the deities or archetypes that align with your path.

## *Building a Relationship with Divine Energies*

**Approaching with Reverence**

When you connect with deities or archetypes, it's essential to approach them with respect and an open heart. Establish a mindset of reverence, acknowledging their power and the role they can play in your life. Creating sacred space can help foster this atmosphere; this might include tidying a corner of your home, setting up an altar, or finding a peaceful outdoor setting where you can connect with these energies.

**Rituals of Connection**
1. **Meditation**: Begin by meditating on the qualities of the deity or archetype you wish to connect with. Visualize inviting their energy into your being, allowing it to fill you with inspiration and guidance.
2. **Dialogue**: Engage in a silent or spoken dialogue. Ask questions and express your thoughts, hopes, or fears. Allow space for the deity or archetype to respond, whether through intuitive feelings or synaptic connections in your mind.
3. **Artistic Expression**: Create art, music, or poetry that resonates with the energy of the deity or archetype. This creative expression can serve as a potent form of connection, allowing you to embody their essence in tangible form.

**Acknowledging Gifts and Lessons**

As you develop your relationship with a deity or archetype, remain mindful of the lessons and insights they offer. Take notes on your experiences and how these energies manifest in your daily life. Celebrate the signs of their presence by incorporating them into your rituals or everyday practices and acknowledge the gifts that come.

## *Rituals for Honoring and Invoking Deities*

**Creating Your Ritual Space**

Start by creating a ritual space that feels sacred to you. This could involve lighting candles, burning incense, arranging flowers, or placing symbols that represent the deity or archetype you wish to honor. Each item serves to invite their presence and enhance the energetic quality of your rituals.

**Example Ritual: Invocation of a Deity**

1. **Preparation**: Gather all your materials, including candles, offerings (flowers, fruits, food), and images or symbols of the deity.
2. **Grounding**: Center yourself through grounding exercises. Breathe deeply, feeling your connection to the Earth, and set the intention for your ritual.
3. **Call to Presence**: Light a candle or incense and recite a prayer or invocation that calls upon the deity to join you. You can find existing prayers or create your own words that express your desire for their presence and guidance.
4. **Offering**: Present your offerings as a gesture of respect and appreciation. You might say something like, "I offer this [item] to honor your divine energy and seek your guidance."
5. **Meditation or Prayer**: Spend time in meditation, asking for clarity, assistance, or inspiration. Allow yourself to receive insights or feelings, remaining open to the ways they might communicate with you.
6. **Closing**: When you feel ready, thank the deity for their presence and support. Snuff out the candles and close the ritual by grounding once more, sealing the energies you've engaged with.

## *Honoring the Divine on a Daily Basis*

Incorporating small rituals into your daily life can help

maintain your relationship with the deities and archetypes you work with. This could be as simple as lighting a candle in their honor, saying a daily affirmation related to the qualities they embody, or reflecting on their teachings during your morning or evening routines.

Working with deities and archetypes offers a profound way to deepen your spiritual practice and enrich your life experience. By intentionally finding the right energies, building relationships with them, and performing rituals of honor and invocation, you invite transformative energies into your everyday life.

Whether through meditation, offering, or creative expression, remember that this journey is a personal and sacred exploration. Trust your intuition, nurture your connections, and allow these divine energies to guide you along your path.

# Chapter 18: Shadow Work

∞∞∞

In the rich tapestry of cottage witchery, where magic intertwines with the mundane, lies an often overlooked but profoundly transformative practice: shadow work. Let's immerse ourselves into the realms of shadow work, its intrinsic connection to personal growth, and how it complements the practice of cottage witchery. Through understanding the deeper aspects of ourselves—the shadows—we can cultivate balance in our lives and align our magical practices with our true selves.

**Understanding Shadow Work within Cottage Witchery**

Shadow work, a term popularized by Jungian psychology, refers to the process of exploring the unconscious aspects of our personality. These 'shadow' traits encompass repressed desires, fears, insecurities, and parts of ourselves that we either ignore or deny. Within cottage witchery, a practice rooted in nature, intuition, and domesticity, shadow work is not just a psychological exercise; it is an essential component of the witch's journey toward holistic self-awareness and empowerment.

Cottage witchery thrives on authenticity—crafting not just spells from foraged herbs, candles, and crystals, but weaving personal truths into every incantation and ritual. The deeper the witch delves into their inner landscape, the richer their magic becomes. Understanding one's shadows opens the door to personal growth, allowing for an authentic connection with the elements of nature, magical energies, and oneself.

To embrace shadow work within cottage witchery, practitioners can start by recognizing the cyclical rhythms of nature—seeing themselves reflected in the phases of the moon, the seasons, and the cycles of life. Just as nature contains both light and dark, so do we. Embracing our entire selves transforms the witch's practice into a profoundly enriching experience, one that invites healing and integration.

## *Techniques for Self-Reflection and Healing*

To embark on the journey of shadow work, one must be equipped with tools for self-reflection and healing. Here are several techniques that can guide the cottage witch in exploring their shadows:

**1. Journaling: The Mirror of the Soul**

Journaling is a powerful tool for uncovering the shadows lurking within. Set aside time to write about your feelings, experiences, and recurring patterns. Approach this with openness; there are no wrong answers here. Consider using prompts like:

- What traits in others irritate me, and what might that reveal about my own shadows?
- In what areas of my life do I feel resistance or fear?
- What recurring themes do I notice in my dreams?

In weaving your thoughts onto the page, you allow your subconscious to speak. This written record not only helps reveal hidden aspects but also serves as a reflection for healing and growth.

## 2. Meditation and Guided Visualization

Meditation can act as a bridge to the shadow self. Find a quiet space, light a candle or some incense, and close your eyes. Allow your breath to guide you to a serene place where you feel safe. Visualize yourself in a dense forest, surrounded by shadows—these shadows represent parts of yourself you have yet to integrate. Observe them without judgment. What do they look like? What emotions do they evoke?

Engage with these shadows. What messages do they hold? As you sit with them, allow feelings to arise. Offer compassion and understanding, acknowledging their presence and allowing them to become part of your wholeness.

## 3. Rituals of Release and Forgiveness

Incorporate shadow work into your rituals. Create a simple ceremony where you honor your shadows. This can involve writing down traits, memories, or experiences you wish to release and then safely burning or burying the paper in nature—a symbolic act of letting go. Follow this with a ritual of forgiveness, either towards yourself or others, using elements such as salt, water, or essential oils to cleanse the space and energy.

## 4. Nature Walks as Reflection

Nature has a unique ability to mirror our inner states. Take intentional walks in your local woods, parks, or gardens. As you walk, reflect on your feelings and observations. What do you notice about the natural world? How does it relate to your own experiences of light and shadow? Document these thoughts in a nature journal, creating a dialogue with the world around you.

## 5. Dream Work

Dreams often reveal unconscious elements of our psyche. Keep a dream journal by your bedside to record your dreams upon waking. Reflect on recurring symbols or narratives and how they may relate to your waking life. Engage with these dreams in your magical practice, using them as guiding insights for your journey within.

## *The Importance of Balance in the Witch's Journey*

In the practice of cottage witchery, balance forms the cornerstone of success and harmony. The journey of exploring one's shadows demands a grounded approach; without balance, the practice can become overwhelming, leading to depression, anxiety, or an aversion to one's own craft.

Embracing both light and dark cultivates a more nuanced perspective on life. It teaches the witch the value of polarity; that joy cannot exist without sorrow, and growth cannot occur without pain. In practicing shadow work, witches learn to navigate life's complexities, weaving them into their spells, rituals, and everyday actions.

Self-care becomes paramount in this journey. Engage in practices that nourish your spirit—be it creating herbal tea blends, tending to your garden, crafting objects of beauty, or simply sitting in silence. Balance also involves recognizing when to draw back from shadow work and focus on building strength and positivity, ensuring that the practice remains a journey toward wholeness rather than a descent into darkness.

Moreover, community matters. Sharing the journey with like-minded practitioners creates a support network to help process emotions and insights. Together, witches can validate each other's experiences, leading to collective healing and growth.

Cottage witchery is not merely a collection of spells and rituals; it is a pathway of continuous personal growth. By embracing shadow work, witches cultivate self-awareness, resilience, and understanding as they navigate their unique paths. Ultimately, the shadows invite us to dance with our fears, reminding us that, like the waxing and waning of the moon, our journey is one of continual balance, growth, and transformation. As practitioners of cottage witchery, we learn to harness the magic within these experiences, cultivating not only our craft but also a truly magical, authentic life.

# Chapter 19: Grounding & Protection Techniques

∞∞∞

In the journey of spiritual and personal growth, grounding and protection are two essential practices that serve as the foundational pillars for any individual seeking strength, stability, and security. Grounding allows us to connect with the Earth and cultivate inner balance, while protection techniques safeguard our energy and environment from negativity. Let's go over some powerful grounding exercises, protective spells and charms specifically for the home, and strategies for creating a daily practice of protection.

## *Grounding Exercises for Maintaining Balance*

Grounding is the act of aligning with the Earth's energy, which not only provides stability but also balances our mental, emotional, and spiritual states. Engaging in grounding exercises can foster a sense of calmness, clarity, and connection. Here are some effective grounding techniques:

### 1. Earth Visualization Meditation

Find a quiet space where you can sit or lie down comfortably. Close your eyes and take several deep breaths, inhaling through your nose and exhaling through your mouth. With each breath, picture yourself becoming more relaxed.

Next, visualize roots extending from your feet into the Earth. Imagine these roots digging deep into the ground, anchoring you to the Earth. Feel the solidness of the Earth beneath you as you draw its energy upward through your roots. Allow this energy to fill your body, creating a sense of warmth and comfort. Repeat affirmations such as *"I am grounded," "I am connected,"* and *"I am strong"* until you feel fully enveloped in the Earth's energy.

## 2. Walking Barefoot

One of the simplest yet most effective ways to ground yourself is to walk barefoot on natural surfaces like grass, soil, or sand. Take a moment to focus on the sensation of each step. Feel the Earth beneath your feet and the textures of the ground. Allow the energy of the Earth to flow into your body, refreshing and revitalizing you. This practice can be especially powerful in natural settings like parks, forests, or beaches.

## 3. Body Scan Meditation

Lay down comfortably and close your eyes. Starting from your toes, bring your awareness to each part of your body, moving slowly up towards your head. Observe any sensations, thoughts, or feelings, without judgment. As you progress, visualize each body part becoming heavier, sinking deeper into the ground. This technique helps to release tension and fosters a deep connection to the present moment.

## 4. Nature Connection

Incorporating nature into your grounding practice can enhance your connection to the Earth. Spend time outdoors, whether it's tending to a garden, sitting by a river, or hiking in the woods.

As you engage with nature, consciously breathe in the fresh air and consciously express gratitude for the beauty and life around you. Allow yourself to be present in the moment, releasing any distractions or worries.

**5. Grounding Stones and Crystals**

Certain stones and crystals are known for their grounding properties, such as hematite, black tourmaline, and smoky quartz. Carrying one of these stones in your pocket or holding it during meditation can help anchor your energy. You might also consider placing these crystals around your home or workspace to promote an environment of balance.

## *Protective Spells and Charms for the Home*

Creating a protective space in your home is essential for maintaining your energetic integrity. Protective spells and charms can act as shields against negative energies and influences. Below are some practical methods for infusing your home with protection.

**1. Salt Protection Ritual**

Salt is a traditional protective agent used across cultures. To create a protective barrier, sprinkle salt around the perimeter of your home, focusing particularly on entrances such as doors and windows. As you do this, visualize a white light forming a protective shield around your living space. Alternatively, you can place small bowls of salt in corners of each room to absorb any stagnant energy.

**2. Protection Spell Jar**

Create a protection jar filled with herbs, stones, and other elements that resonate with you. Consider combining ingredients such as rosemary (for protection), black salt (for banishing negativity), and a small piece of quartz (to amplify energy). As you layer each ingredient, focus on your intent for protection, affirming, "*This jar protects my home from all negativity.*" Seal the jar with wax or a lid and place it in a discreet location in your home.

### 3. Protective Amulet Crafting

Crafting an amulet can be a personal and powerful act of protection. Gather materials that resonate with you, such as stones, feathers, or symbols of protection (like the eye of Horus or pentacle). As you assemble your amulet, visualize it absorbing negativity and deflecting harmful influences. Keep the amulet in your home, hang it above an entrance, or wear it as jewelry for personal protection.

### 4. Cleansing and Blessing Rituals

Regularly cleansing your home of stagnant or negative energy can enhance protective measures. Use sage, palo santo, or cedar to smudge your space while setting the intention for protection. As you do this, visualize white light filling each room. You may also incorporate sound to cleanse and elevate the energy—ringing bells or using singing bowls can enhance the effect.

### 5. Protective Crystals for the Home

Incorporate protective crystals throughout your home. Clear quartz can amplify positive energy, while black tourmaline is known for absorbing electromagnetic and psychic burdens. Place these crystals near entrances, windows, or in living spaces to enhance the protection and promote a harmonious environment.

## *Creating a Daily Practice of Protection*

To ensure ongoing protection and balance, integrating a daily practice focused on these techniques can be immensely beneficial. Here are several ways to cultivate this routine:

**1. Morning Grounding Routine**

Start your day with a grounding routine that reconnects you with the Earth. Upon waking, take a moment to sit on the edge of your bed, place your feet on the floor, and visualize grounding roots. Breathe deeply as you express gratitude for the day ahead. This grounding exercise will set a positive tone for your day.

**2. Affirmations for Protection**

Incorporate protective affirmations into your daily routine. Consider statements such as *"I am protected and safe,"* *"I attract only positive energy,"* or *"My home is a sanctuary filled with love and light."* Repeat these phrases in the morning, throughout the day, or before sleeping to reinforce your protective energy.

**3. Evening Cleansing Ritual**

Create a wind-down ritual that incorporates cleansing and protection practices. This can include lighting a candle, burning incense, or using essential oils while reflecting on your day. Visualize releasing any negativity gathered throughout the day and reinforce your protective shield around yourself and your home.

**4. Weekly Energy Checks**

Set aside time each week to check in with your energy and your living space. Reflect on how you've been feeling and if there are any areas of your home that need cleansing or added protective measures. You can even create a dedicated space for protection rituals, enrich it with meaningful objects, and charge it with your intention.

**5. Gratitude Practice**

Incorporate gratitude into your daily life. Regularly acknowledging the positives creates a shield against negativity and invites more abundance into your life. Consider keeping a gratitude journal where you pen down the things you are thankful for each day, including the protection you feel in your home.

By integrating these grounding and protective techniques into your life, you create a robust framework that allows you to thrive amidst life's challenges. Grounding provides a sense of stability, while protection empowers you to navigate the world with confidence. As you maintain a harmonious balance between these practices, you will find that not only do you remain stable and secure, but you also cultivate a space where joy and peace can flourish.

# Chapter 20: Remedies & Recipes

In the heart of every cottage witch lies a deep connection to nature and an understanding of the healing properties found within the herbs, flowers, and other natural ingredients that grow around us. I've provided a collection of homemade remedies and recipes that you can easily craft in your own kitchen, blending traditional knowledge with the energy of your personal intuition. To be a true cottage witch is to embrace simplicity, creativity, and the wisdom of the earth.

# 1. Herbal Infusions & Teas

### A. Calming Chamomile Tea

**Ingredients:**
- 2 tablespoons dried chamomile flowers
- 1 teaspoon honey (optional)
- 2 cups boiling water

**Instructions:**
1. In a teapot or heat-proof container, add the dried chamomile flowers.
2. Pour boiling water over the flowers and steep for about 10 minutes.
3. Strain the tea into a cup, add honey if desired, and enjoy the soothing effects.

**Uses:** This tea is perfect for relaxation and can help reduce anxiety and promote sleep.

### B. Revitalizing Peppermint Tea

**Ingredients:**
- 1 tablespoon dried peppermint leaves
- 1 teaspoon honey or agave syrup (optional)
- 2 cups boiling water

**Instructions:**
1. Place dried peppermint leaves in a teapot or cup.
2. Pour boiling water over the leaves and let steep for 5-7 minutes.
3. Strain, sweeten to taste, and enjoy the invigorating flavor.

**Uses:** Peppermint tea is great for digestion and can help relieve headaches.

# 2. Healing Salves

## A. Lavender Infused Healing Salve

**Ingredients:**

- 1 cup olive oil
- 1/4 cup dried lavender flowers
- 1/4 cup beeswax pastilles

**Instructions:**

1. In a double boiler, combine olive oil and dried lavender. Heat gently for 2 hours, allowing the lavender to infuse.
2. Strain the oil through cheesecloth to remove the flowers.
3. Return the infused oil to the double boiler and add beeswax. Stir until melted.
4. Pour the mixture into small jars and let it cool to solidify.

**Uses:** This salve is perfect for soothing skin irritations, minor burns, and cuts.

## B. Comfrey and Calendula Salve

**Ingredients:**

- 1 cup olive oil
- 1/4 cup dried comfrey root
- 1/4 cup dried calendula petals
- 1/4 cup beeswax pastilles

**Instructions:**

1. In a double boiler, combine olive oil, comfrey root, and calendula petals. Heat gently for 2 hours.
2. Strain the mixture through a fine mesh cloth or cheesecloth.
3. Return the oil to the double boiler, add beeswax, and stir until melted.
4. Pour into jars and let cool.

**Uses:** This salve helps with bruises, sprains, and skin healing, thanks to the properties of comfrey and calendula.

## *C. Headache Salve*

**Ingredients:**

- 1 cup carrier oil (such as jojoba oil, sweet almond oil, or olive oil)
- 1/4 cup dried lavender flowers
- 1/4 cup dried peppermint leaves (or 10-15 drops of peppermint essential oil)
- 1/4 cup beeswax pastilles
- 10 drops of eucalyptus essential oil (optional, for an additional cooling effect)

**Instructions:**

1. **Infuse the Carrier Oil:** In a double boiler, combine the carrier oil, dried lavender flowers, and dried peppermint leaves. Heat gently for 1-2 hours on low,

stirring occasionally. This process allows the healing properties of the herbs to infuse into the oil.

2. **Strain the Mixture:** After infusing, strain the oil through a fine mesh strainer or cheesecloth to remove the solid herbs. Be sure to press down on the herbs to extract as much oil as possible.

3. **Melt the Beeswax:** Return the infused oil to the double boiler and add the beeswax pastilles. Stir gently until the beeswax is melted and blended with the oil.

4. **Add Essential Oils:** If desired, add the eucalyptus essential oil and stir well to combine.

5. **Pour and Cool:** Pour the mixture into small jars or tins while still warm. Allow the salve to cool completely and solidify.

**Uses:** When a headache strikes, roll a small amount of the salve onto your temples and the back of your neck. The combined properties of lavender and peppermint can help reduce tension and soothe discomfort. The eucalyptus adds a refreshing touch that enhances the cooling effect.

# 3. Essential Oil Blends

## A. Calming Lavender Roll-On

**Ingredients:**
- 10 drops lavender essential oil
- 5 drops frankincense essential oil
- 2 tablespoons carrier oil (like sweet almond or jojoba oil)

**Instructions:**
1. In a small glass roller bottle, combine essential oils with the carrier oil.
2. Roll onto pulse points when you need calming energy.

**Uses:** This blend is perfect for stress relief and promoting restful sleep.

## B. Refreshing Citrus Mist

**Ingredients:**
- 10 drops sweet orange essential oil
- 5 drops lemon essential oil
- 2 cups distilled water

**Instructions:**
1. In a spray bottle, combine essential oils and distilled

water.

2. Shake well before each use and spray around your living space for a refreshing aroma.

**Uses:** This mist can uplift your mood and purify the air in your home.

# 4. Bath Soaks & Scrubs

## A. Relaxing Rose Petal Bath Soak

**Ingredients:**
- 1 cup Epsom salt
- 1/2 cup sea salt
- 1/2 cup dried rose petals
- 10 drops rose essential oil

**Instructions:**
1. In a bowl, combine Epsom salt, sea salt, and dried rose petals.
2. Add essential oil and mix well.
3. Store in a glass jar and use 1/2 cup per bath.

**Uses:** This soak relaxes the body, softens the skin, and lifts the spirit.

## B. Exfoliating Coffee Scrub

**Ingredients:**
- 1 cup used coffee grounds
- 1/2 cup coconut oil
- 1/2 cup brown sugar
- 1 teaspoon vanilla extract

**Instructions:**

1. In a bowl, mix together all ingredients until well combined.
2. Store in an airtight container and use in the shower.

**Uses:** This scrub exfoliates, hydrates, and awakens the senses with its rich aroma.

# 5. Tinctures & Extracts

## A. Herbal Immune Tincture

**Ingredients:**
- 1 cup dried echinacea root
- 1 cup dried elderberries
- 2 cups vodka (or apple cider vinegar for a non-alcoholic version)

**Instructions:**
1. Place dried echinacea and elderberries in a mason jar.
2. Fill with vodka, ensuring herbs are fully submerged.
3. Seal the jar and shake gently. Store in a cool, dark place for 4-6 weeks, shaking occasionally.
4. After the infusion period, strain into a dropper bottle.

**Uses:** Take a few drops during cold season to bolster your immune system.

## B. Vanilla Extract

**Ingredients:**
- 5-8 vanilla beans
- 1 cup vodka or rum

**Instructions:**

1. Split the vanilla beans down the center and place in a glass jar.
2. Pour vodka or rum over the beans, ensuring they are fully submerged.
3. Seal and store in a cool, dark place for at least 8 weeks, shaking occasionally.

**Uses:** This rich extract can be used in baking and cooking, infusing your creations with delightful flavor.

# 6. Magical Infusions

### A. Protective Rosemary Water

**Ingredients:**
- 1 cup fresh rosemary sprigs
- 2 cups boiling water

**Instructions:**
1. Place rosemary in a heatproof container.
2. Pour boiling water over the rosemary and let steep for 20 minutes.
3. Strain and store the liquid in a spray bottle.

**Uses:** Use this spray to cleanse spaces and objects of negative energy, invoking protection.

### B. Love-Boosting Rose Quartz Water

**Ingredients:**
- 1-2 small rose quartz crystals (ensure they are safe for water)
- 1 liter of water

**Instructions:**
1. Cleanse your rose quartz crystals under running water.
2. Place them in a jar filled with water and allow them to

infuse for at least 4 hours.
3. Drink the water or use it in your rituals to attract love.

**Uses:** This enchanted water can be used internally to boost self-love or externally in rituals to attract romantic energy.

As a cottage witch, these homemade remedies and recipes serve not only as practical solutions but also as a means of welcoming nature's magic into your daily life. Each product you create is infused with your intention and energy, making it a unique addition to your apothecary.

Remember that the journey of a cottage witch is always evolving; feel free to experiment, infuse your own magical intentions, and enjoy the alchemy of creation. Your potions, teas, and remedies are not just for healing—they are a celebration of the ever-present bond between you, your craft, and the natural world.

# 7. Crafting Homemade Candles

Candles hold a special place in the cottage witch's practice. They not only provide light and warmth but also serve as magical tools for intention setting, meditation, and enhancing the ambiance of your sacred space. By crafting your own candles, you can infuse them with personal intention, essential oils, herbs, and crystals, crafting a unique tool tailored to your desires. This section will guide you through the process of making simple homemade candles, as well as provide recipes for specific purposes.

## A. Basic Candle Making Supplies

**Ingredients:**
- Wax (beeswax, soy wax, or palm wax)
- Wick (cotton or wooden wicks)
- Essential oils or fragrance oils (optional)
- Color dye (optional, especially for soy wax)
- Herbs, flowers, or crystals (optional)

**Tools:**
- Double boiler or a pot for melting wax
- Thermometer
- Candle molds or jars
- Stirring utensil

- Wick holder or pencil (to keep the wick centered)
- Pouring pitcher

## *B. Classic Beeswax Candles*

**Instructions:**

1. **Prepare Your Work Area:** Lay down newspaper or a protective covering, as candle-making can be a bit messy.

2. **Melt the Wax:** Using a double boiler, melt beeswax gently over low to medium heat until it reaches about 145°F (63°C). Stir occasionally to ensure even melting.

3. **Prepare the Wick:** While the wax melts, secure the wick in the center of your mold or jar. If using a mold, you can use a wick holder or pencil across the top to keep it centered.

4. **Add Essential Oils (Optional):** Once the wax is melted, remove it from the heat. If you choose to customize your candles, add essential oils (about 1 ounce per pound of wax) and stir well.

5. **Pour the Wax:** Carefully pour the melted wax into the prepared mold or jar, making sure not to disturb the wick.

6. **Cool and Trim:** Allow the candle to cool completely, which usually takes a few hours. Once cooled, trim the wick to about 1/4 inch above the wax surface.

7. **Curing:** For the best scent throw, allow your candles to cure for 48 hours before burning them.

**Uses:** These beeswax candles burn cleanly and emit a natural honey scent. Light them during meditation or ritual to enhance your practice.

## C. Scented Soy Candles with Herbal Infusions

**Instructions:**

1. **Prepare Your Work Area:** Lay down protective covering for your workspace.
2. **Melt the Soy Wax:** As before, use a double boiler to melt soy wax. Heat it to around 170°F (77°C).
3. **Infuse with Herbs:** While the wax melts, prepare your herbs. You might choose dried lavender for relaxation or rosemary for clarity. You can place these herbs in a small pouch or add them directly to the melted wax.
4. **Add Essential Oils:** When the wax reaches 170°F, remove it from the heat. Add essential oils of your choice (the same measurement as beeswax) and blend thoroughly.
5. **Pour and Cool:** Follow the same pouring and cooling procedure as with beeswax candles, securing the wick before pouring.
6. **Optional Coloring:** If you want to add color, you can mix in soy candle dye or use natural coloring agents like turmeric for a warm hue.
7. **Trim and Cure:** Once cooled, trim the wick and cure for a couple of days.

**Uses:** Soy candles burn longer than beeswax and hold scent beautifully. They can be used for self-care rituals, enhancing the atmosphere for relaxation, or creating a romantic setting.

## D. Intention Candles

### 1. Protection Candle

**Ingredients:**
- 1 cup soy wax
- Black dye (for color)
- 10 drops of protection essential oils (like frankincense or cedarwood)
- Dried rosemary and black tourmaline crystal chips

**Instructions:**
1. Melt the soy wax.
2. Add black dye until the desired color is achieved.
3. Stir in essential oils and infused herbs/crystals.
4. Pour into a prepped jar with a wick and allow to cool.

**Uses:** Light this candle when you need to create a protective shield around yourself or your home.

## *2. Love Attraction Candle*

**Ingredients:**
- 1 cup beeswax or soy wax
- Pink or red dye
- 10 drops of essential oils (like lavender, rose, or ylang-ylang)
- Dried rose petals and a small rose quartz crystal

**Instructions:**
1. Follow the same melting procedure with the wax.
2. Add the dye and essential oils after melting, stirring well.
3. Incorporate the dried rose petals and tuck in the rose quartz before pouring.

**Uses:** Light this candle during rituals focused on love, self-acceptance, or attracting romance into your life.

### 3. Clarity and Focus Candle
**Ingredients:**
- 1 cup soy wax
- Yellow dye
- 10 drops of clarity-enhancing oils (like lemon or peppermint)
- Dried lemon balm and clear quartz pieces

**Instructions:**
1. Melt the wax as previously described, adding dye and oils once melted.
2. Stir in the herbs and quartz before pouring.

**Uses:** Use this candle when studying, working, or needing mental clarity.

## E. Candle Care and Tradition

- **Anointing Candles**: Anoint your candles with oils that correspond to your intention. Use your dominant hand to lightly rub oil from the bottom of the candle towards the top, sealing your intention into the candle.
- **Personalizing Your Candles**: Before burning, feel free to take a moment to meditate on your intention for the candle. Write it down, state it aloud, or visualize your desire as you light the wick.
- **Safety First**: Always burn candles in a safe environment. Keep them away from drafts, flammable materials, and never leave them unattended.

Candle-making is an art that connects the cottage witch to the elements of fire, earth, and choice. By taking the time to create personalized candles, you amplify your intentions and bring an extra layer of magic to your witchcraft. Whether for self-care or magic, these candles serve as tools to illuminate your path, enhance rituals, and add warmth to your home. Embrace this craft and watch your intentions light the way.

# 8. Homemade Laundry Solutions

As home and hearth are central to the practice of a cottage witch, maintaining a clean and harmonious living space is vital. Using homemade laundry soap, fabric softener, and dryer balls not only reduces your reliance on commercial products but also infuses your laundry with natural ingredients that can be empowered with intention. This section presents simple recipes for creating your own laundry soap, fabric softener, and dryer balls, allowing you to keep your garments fresh while embracing sustainability.

## A. Homemade Laundry Soap

**Ingredients:**

- 1 bar of soap (such as Castile soap, Fels-Naptha, or any natural soap you prefer)
- 1 cup washing soda (sodium carbonate, not baking soda)
- 1 cup borax (optional, for stain removal and brightening)

**Instructions:**

1. **Grate the Soap:** Using a cheese grater or food processor, finely grate the bar of soap until you have a uniform texture.
2. **Mix the Ingredients:** In a large bowl, combine the grated soap, washing soda, and borax. Stir well until

fully blended.

3. **Store:** Transfer the mixture into an airtight container, such as a glass jar or a plastic tub with a lid.
4. **Use:** Add 1-2 tablespoons of the mixture to each load of laundry, adjusting based on the size and soil level of your laundry.

**Optional Additives:**

- For scent, consider adding 10-20 drops of your favorite essential oil (such as lavender, lemongrass, or eucalyptus) to the dry mixture before storing.
- Dried herbs like lavender or rosemary can also be included for a gentle scent and natural antibacterial properties.

**Uses:** This homemade laundry soap effectively cleans clothes without harsh chemicals. It's especially beneficial for sensitive skin or for those looking to reduce their environmental footprint.

## *B. Natural Fabric Softener*

**Ingredients:**

- 1 cup white vinegar
- 1 cup water
- 10-15 drops of essential oil (such as lavender, lemon, or chamomile)

**Instructions:**

1. **Combine Ingredients:** In a clean spray bottle or mixing bowl, combine the white vinegar and water.
2. **Add Essential Oils:** Drop in the essential oil(s) of your choice, and mix well to ensure an even distribution.

3. **Store:** Keep the mixture in the spray bottle or pour it into a glass jar.

**Usage:**

- For each load of laundry, add about ½ cup of the fabric softener to the rinse cycle. If using a spray bottle, spray directly onto clothes as they spin in the rinse cycle.

**Benefits:** This natural fabric softener helps to reduce static cling and softens fabrics without the use of synthetic chemicals. The vinegar also acts as a natural deodorizer, helping to eliminate any lingering odors.

## *C. DIY Dryer Balls*

**Materials:**

- 100% wool yarn (or you can purchase pre-made wool dryer balls)
- Pantyhose or an old stocking (if making your own)

**Instructions:**

1. **Create the Balls:** If using wool yarn, start by wrapping the yarn around your fingers about 25-30 times to create a small bundle. Remove it from your fingers and wrap more yarn around it to create a ball shape. Continue wrapping tightly until the ball is about the size of a tennis ball.
2. **Secure the Balls:** Use a small piece of yarn to tie off the end of the wrapped ball to keep it intact.
3. **Felt the Balls:** Place your yarn balls in a pantyhose or old stocking, tying knots between each ball to keep them from touching one another. Wash and dry them on hot settings to help felt the wool (which will strengthen the balls).

4. **Remove and Use:** Once cooled, remove the felted balls from the pantyhose. You can make multiple dryer balls to maximize the effectiveness.

**Optional Perfuming:**

- If desired, add a few drops of your favorite essential oil to each dryer ball before tossing them into the dryer. A blend of lavender and lemon can create a refreshing scent.

**Usage:** Toss 2-4 balls into your dryer with each load. They help to separate clothes, which speeds up drying time and reduces static cling.

**Benefits:** Wool dryer balls are a natural alternative to commercial dryer sheets, softening fabrics while being reusable. They can last for years with proper care, making them an eco-friendly choice.

Creating your own laundry solutions is a satisfying and eco-conscious way to harness the magic and intention of your home. By using homemade laundry soap, natural fabric softeners, and wool dryer balls, you infuse your clothing and linens with love, care, and the energy of your chosen herbs and essential oils.

This not only promotes a cleaner home but also enhances the overall atmosphere of your living space, reflecting the harmony and creativity inherent in cottage witchcraft. Embrace these practices as part of your routine and let your laundry area become a delightful sanctuary of freshness and intention.

# 9. Homemade Beauty Products

Crafting your own beauty products is a wonderful way to care for your skin and hair using natural ingredients that align with the principles of cottage witchcraft. Not only do homemade beauty products avoid synthetic chemicals and fragrances, but they also allow you to infuse your creations with personal intention, herbal magic, and the scents that resonate with your spirit. This section will guide you through recipes for lotions, buttercreams, whipped body butter, lip balms, and hair care products, all crafted with love and care.

## A. Nourishing Lotion

**Ingredients:**

- 1/2 cup distilled water or herbal infusion (like chamomile or lavender)
- 1/4 cup almond oil or jojoba oil
- 1/4 cup emulsifying wax
- 1 tablespoon shea butter or cocoa butter
- 10-15 drops essential oils (such as lavender, geranium, or ylang-ylang)

**Instructions:**

1. **Prepare a Double Boiler:** Fill a saucepan with a few inches of water and place over low heat. In a heat-proof bowl, combine the emulsifying wax, almond oil, and

shea/cocoa butter.

2. **Melt Ingredients:** Stir the mixture until melted and fully combined, then remove from heat.
3. **Combine Water and Oils:** In a separate container, heat the distilled water or herbal infusion until warm (not boiling).
4. **Blend Together:** Slowly pour the warm water into the oil mixture, whisking continuously for several minutes until fully emulsified.
5. **Add Essential Oils:** Once cooled, add in your chosen essential oils and mix well.
6. **Store:** Transfer the lotion into sterilized glass jars or bottles and let cool completely.

**Uses:** This lightweight lotion hydrates and nourishes the skin while providing a delightful aromatherapy experience.

## *B. Whipped Body Butter*

**Ingredients:**

- 1/2 cup shea butter
- 1/2 cup coconut oil
- 1/4 cup sweet almond oil or olive oil
- 10-15 drops essential oil of your choice (such as lavender or citrus)

**Instructions:**

1. **Melt Base Ingredients:** In a double boiler, combine shea butter and coconut oil, stirring until melted.
2. **Cool Slightly:** Allow the mixture to cool slightly at room temperature until it starts to solidify but remains pliable.

3. **Whip it Up:** Using a hand mixer or stand mixer, whip the mixture for about 5-10 minutes until it becomes fluffy and light.
4. **Add Oils:** Gradually incorporate the sweet almond or olive oil and essential oils while continuing to whip until fully combined.
5. **Store:** Spoon the whipped body butter into clean, airtight containers.

**Uses:** This luxurious body butter deeply hydrates and nourishes the skin, making it perfect for dry areas like elbows and knees or as an all-over moisturizer.

## C. Homemade Lip Balm

**Ingredients:**
- 1 tablespoon beeswax pastilles
- 2 tablespoons coconut oil
- 2 tablespoons sweet almond oil (or olive oil)
- 10 drops of flavored oil (like peppermint or vanilla) or essential oil

**Instructions:**
1. **Melt Ingredients:** In a double boiler, melt the beeswax, coconut oil, and sweet almond oil together until fully liquid.
2. **Remove from Heat:** Remove the mixture from heat and allow to cool briefly.
3. **Add Flavoring:** Stir in your desired flavored or essential oils.
4. **Pour into Containers:** Carefully pour the mixture into lip balm tubes or small tins before it solidifies.

5. **Cool Completely:** Allow the lip balm to cool and harden fully before use.

**Uses:** This nourishing lip balm protects and softens lips while leaving them with a gentle, pleasant scent or flavor.

## *D. Herbal Hair Rinse*

**Ingredients:**

- 2 cups water
- 1/2 cup dried herbs (choose based on hair type; rosemary for oily hair, chamomile for blonde hair, or nettle for overall health)
- 1 tablespoon apple cider vinegar (optional, for shine)

**Instructions:**

1. **Prepare Herbal Infusion:** Bring the water to a boil, then add the dried herbs. Remove from heat and let it steep for at least 30 minutes.
2. **Strain:** Strain the herbal infusion into a clean container, discarding the herbs.
3. **Add Vinegar:** If using, mix in the apple cider vinegar.
4. **Use:** After shampooing, pour this rinse over your hair, massaging it into the scalp and hair. Leave it on for a few minutes before rinsing with cool water.

**Benefits:** Herbal rinses can enhance shine, balance oil, and promote scalp health, depending on the herbs used.

## *E. Hair Conditioning Mask*

**Ingredients:**

- 1 ripe avocado

- 2 tablespoons coconut oil
- 1 tablespoon honey

**Instructions:**

1. **Blend Ingredients:** In a bowl, mash the avocado until smooth. Mix in coconut oil and honey until well combined.
2. **Apply to Hair:** On clean, damp hair, apply the mixture generously from roots to ends.
3. **Leave On:** Cover your hair with a shower cap and let the mask sit for 20-30 minutes.
4. **Rinse and Shampoo:** Rinse thoroughly and follow with a gentle shampoo if desired.

**Uses:** This nourishing mask revitalizes dry and damaged hair, leaving it soft and manageable.

Creating your own beauty products not only allows you to customize what you apply to your skin and hair but also connects you deeply with the magical properties of the ingredients you choose. Each recipe serves as an expression of your craft, made with intention and love rooted in nature.

Whether crafting a luxurious body butter, nurturing lip balm, or herbal hair treatment, these homemade products will not only enhance your beauty ritual but also bring a touch of magic into your daily life. Embrace the alchemy of homemade beauty and let the power of nature nourish your body and soul.

# 10. Homemade Perfumes

Creating your own perfumes, whether in solid or roll-on form, is a delightful way to capture your essence and express your individuality. Using natural ingredients allows you to customize scents to reflect your mood, intentions, and the energy surrounding you. This section will guide you through two methods of crafting homemade perfumes—solid perfumes and roll-on perfumes—using essential oils and carrier oils that resonate with your spirit.

## A. Solid Perfume

**Ingredients:**

- 1 tablespoon beeswax pastilles
- 1 tablespoon shea butter or coconut oil
- 2 tablespoons jojoba oil or sweet almond oil
- 15-30 drops essential oils (your preferred blend)

**Instructions:**

1. **Melt the Base Ingredients:** Using a double boiler, combine the beeswax pastilles, shea butter (or coconut oil), and jojoba oil. Heat gently until fully melted and mixed.
2. **Add Essential Oils:** Remove the mixture from heat and allow it to cool slightly (not too long, as it will begin to solidify). Add your chosen essential oils, blending

them to create your desired scent. This can be a single oil or a combination—experiment to find what you love!

3. **Pour into Containers:** Once mixed, quickly pour the liquid into small tins or containers while still warm. Allow to cool completely until solidified.

4. **Set Intention (Optional):** As the perfume solidifies, take a moment to set your intention for the scent. Visualize how you wish to embody that fragrance energy.

**Uses:** Solid perfumes are perfect for travel or on-the-go applications. Simply rub a small amount on your wrist, pulse points, or behind your ears for a lasting scent.

## B. Roll-On Perfume

**Ingredients:**

- 2 tablespoons carrier oil (such as jojoba oil, sweet almond oil, or fractionated coconut oil)
- 10-20 drops essential oils (your preferred blend)
- 10-15 ml glass roller bottle

**Instructions:**

1. **Prepare the Bottle:** If desired, before filling, add a couple of small crystals (such as rose quartz for love or clear quartz for clarity) to your roller bottle for added intention and energy.

2. **Combine Oils:** In a small measuring cup or directly in your glass roller bottle, combine the carrier oil with the essential oils. Adjust the number of drops depending on how strong you want the scent to be. Start with fewer drops and build the scent to your preference.

3. **Mix Well:** Secure the rollerball top onto the bottle and shake gently to mix. Let it sit for at least an hour (or up to 24 hours) to allow the scents to meld.
4. **Set Intention (Optional):** As you mix, take a moment to breathe in the aroma and set your intention for how you'd like to use or embody this fragrance.

**Uses:** Roll-on perfumes are easy to apply and ideal for refreshment throughout the day. Apply to pulse points, such as wrists, neck, or behind ears, for a pleasing, personalized fragrance experience.

## C. Suggested Essential Oil Blends

*1. Calming Lavender & Chamomile Blend*
- 15 drops lavender essential oil
- 10 drops chamomile essential oil

*2. Uplifting Citrus Blend*
- 10 drops sweet orange essential oil
- 5 drops lemon essential oil
- 5 drops bergamot essential oil

*3. Grounding Earthy Blend*
- 10 drops cedarwood essential oil
- 10 drops patchouli essential oil
- 5 drops frankincense essential oil

*4. Romantic Floral Blend*
- 10 drops rose essential oil
- 10 drops geranium essential oil
- 5 drops ylang-ylang essential oil

Creating your own perfumes, whether in solid or roll-on form, allows you to embrace the power of scent as a tool for self-expression, meditation, and intention-setting. These homemade fragrances celebrate your uniqueness while harnessing the healing properties of essential oils.

As a cottage witch, you can infuse your perfumes with energy and purpose, making each application a magical ritual in its own right. Enjoy experimenting with different combinations and let your personality shine through in every fragrant creation.

# Chapter 21: Sabbat Recipes

∞∞∞

As the wheel of the year turns, the Sabbats offer a rich tapestry of celebration, connection, and reflection for the cottage witch. Each festival provides an opportunity to honor the changing seasons, the abundance of nature, and the cycles of life and death. Below you will find some delightful recipes that capture the essence of the season.

**Introduction to the Wheel of the Year**

The Wheel of the Year is marked by eight Sabbats, each corresponding to a significant seasonal change and tied to ancient traditions. As a cottage witch, celebrating these Sabbats brings you closer to nature and allows you to cultivate a deeper understanding of your craft. Each celebration can be enriched through rituals, decorations, and, importantly, food.

# Samhain (October 31 - November 1)

**Significance:** Samhain marks the end of the harvest and the beginning of winter. It is a time when the veil between the worlds is thinnest, allowing for communication with ancestors.

## 1. Roasted Pumpkin Soup

**Ingredients:**

- 1 medium pumpkin (about 3-4 pounds), halved and seeds removed
- 2 tablespoons olive oil
- 1 onion, chopped
- 3 garlic cloves, minced
- 4 cups vegetable broth
- 1 teaspoon ground cinnamon
- 1/2 teaspoon nutmeg
- Salt and pepper to taste
- 1/2 cup cream or coconut milk (optional)
- Pumpkin seeds for garnish

**Instructions:**

1. Preheat your oven to 400°F (200°C).
2. Brush the cut sides of the pumpkin with olive oil and place them cut-side down on a baking sheet. Roast for about 45 minutes, or until tender.
3. In a large pot, heat the remaining olive oil over

medium heat. Add the onion and garlic and sauté until softened, about 5 minutes.

4. Scoop the flesh from the roasted pumpkin and add it to the pot. Pour in the vegetable broth, and add cinnamon, nutmeg, salt, and pepper.
5. Bring the mixture to a simmer and cook for about 10-15 minutes. Blend with an immersion blender (or transfer to a blender) until smooth.
6. Stir in cream or coconut milk if desired, and blend again if needed. Serve hot, garnished with pumpkin seeds.

## *2. Apple Cider with Spices*

**Ingredients:**
- 1 gallon apple cider
- 4 cinnamon sticks
- 5-6 whole cloves
- 1 tablespoon whole allspice
- Zest of 1 orange
- 1 tablespoon brown sugar (optional)

**Instructions:**

1. In a large pot, combine the apple cider, cinnamon sticks, cloves, allspice, and orange zest.
2. Heat over medium heat until it reaches a simmer. Reduce the heat and let it simmer for 30-40 minutes to allow the flavors to meld.
3. If desired, add brown sugar to sweeten. Strain out the spices and serve warm.

## 3. Brown Bread with Honey and Nuts

**Ingredients:**

- 2 cups whole wheat flour
- 1 cup all-purpose flour
- 1/4 cup brown sugar
- 1 teaspoon baking soda
- 1 teaspoon baking powder
- 1/2 teaspoon salt
- 1/4 cup honey
- 1 1/2 cups buttermilk
- 1/2 cup mixed nuts (walnuts, pecans, or hazelnuts), chopped

**Instructions:**

1. Preheat your oven to 350°F (175°C). Grease a 9x5-inch loaf pan.
2. In a large bowl, mix the whole wheat flour, all-purpose flour, brown sugar, baking soda, baking powder, and salt.
3. In another bowl, combine honey with buttermilk until well mixed. Pour this mixture into the dry ingredients and stir until just combined. Fold in the chopped nuts.
4. Pour the batter into the prepared loaf pan and bake for 50-60 minutes, or until a toothpick inserted into the center comes out clean.
5. Let cool for 10 minutes in the pan before transferring to a wire rack. Slice and serve with more honey for drizzling.

## 4. Traditional Colcannon

**Ingredients:**
- 2 pounds potatoes, peeled and cubed
- 1 cup kale or cabbage, chopped
- 1/4 cup milk or cream
- 4 tablespoons butter
- Salt and pepper to taste
- 2-3 green onions, chopped

**Instructions:**
1. Boil potatoes in a large pot of salted water until tender, about 15-20 minutes.
2. In another pot, add the chopped kale or cabbage to boiling water and cook for 3-5 minutes until tender. Drain and set aside.
3. Once the potatoes are tender, drain and return them to the pot. Add the milk or cream and 2 tablespoons of butter, mashing until smooth.
4. Stir in the cooked kale or cabbage, green onions, and season with salt and pepper. Serve with additional butter on top.

## *5. Witch's Brew Punch*

**Ingredients:**
- 4 cups grape juice
- 4 cups cranberry juice
- 2 cups sparkling water or ginger ale
- 1 orange, sliced
- 1 lemon, sliced
- 1 lime, sliced

- Optional: gummy worms or candy eyeballs for garnish

**Instructions:**
1. In a large punch bowl, combine grape juice, cranberry juice, and sparkling water or ginger ale.
2. Add the sliced fruits for a festive touch. If you like, toss in gummy worms or candy eyeballs.
3. Stir gently and serve over ice for a refreshing, witchy drink.

These recipes are perfect for a Samhain celebration, evoking the flavors of the season while allowing for a warm and welcoming atmosphere among friends and family. Enjoy!

# Yule (Winter Solstice - December 21)

**Significance:** Yule celebrates the rebirth of the sun. It is a time of reflection, renewal, and hope as the days begin to lengthen.

### 1. Yule Log Cake (Bûche de Noël)

**Ingredients:**
- **For the sponge cake:**
- 4 large eggs
- 1/2 cup granulated sugar
- 1/3 cup all-purpose flour
- 1/3 cup cocoa powder
- 1/4 teaspoon salt
- 1 teaspoon vanilla extract
- **For the filling:**
- 1 cup heavy cream
- 2 tablespoons powdered sugar
- 1 teaspoon vanilla extract
- **For the chocolate ganache:**
- 8 oz. dark chocolate, chopped
- 1/2 cup heavy cream

**Instructions:**

1. **Preheat the oven** to 350°F (175°C). Grease and line a 15x10 inch jelly roll pan with parchment paper.
2. **Make the sponge:** In a bowl, beat the eggs and sugar until light and fluffy. Gradually fold in the flour, cocoa powder, and salt, then add vanilla.
3. **Spread the batter** evenly in the prepared pan and bake for 12-15 minutes or until a toothpick comes out clean.
4. Once baked, turn the cake out onto a clean kitchen towel sprinkled with powdered sugar. Roll the cake (with the towel) into a log shape and let it cool completely.
5. **Prepare the filling:** Whip the cream with powdered sugar and vanilla until soft peaks form. Unroll the cake and spread the filling evenly.
6. Roll the cake back into a log without the towel, then cut a small piece from one end to create the "branch" effect.
7. **Make the ganache:** Heat the cream until just boiling, then pour it over the chopped chocolate. Let it sit for 5 minutes and stir until smooth.
8. **Decorate:** Place the log on a serving platter, cover with ganache, and use a fork to make bark-like patterns. Dust with powdered sugar and decorate with holly or other festive garnishes.

## *2. Herb-Infused Mulled Wine*

**Ingredients:**

- 1 bottle red wine (Merlot or Cabernet Sauvignon)
- 1/4 cup honey or sugar (to taste)
- 1 orange, sliced
- 4 whole cloves

- 2 star anise
- 3 cinnamon sticks
- 1 piece of fresh ginger (about 1 inch), sliced
- 2 cups apple cider

**Instructions:**

1. In a large pot, combine the red wine, honey (or sugar), apple cider, orange slices, cloves, star anise, cinnamon sticks, and ginger.
2. Heat over low to medium heat, stirring occasionally until warm. Do not boil as this will evaporate the alcohol.
3. Once heated through, let the mixture simmer on low for about 30 minutes to an hour for the flavors to meld.
4. Strain the mixture into mugs, removing the spices and orange slices. Garnish with an additional cinnamon stick or a slice of orange.
5. Serve warm and enjoy!

## 3. Winter Root Vegetable Soup

**Ingredients:**

- 2 tablespoons olive oil
- 1 onion, chopped
- 2 carrots, chopped
- 2 parsnips, chopped
- 1 sweet potato, diced
- 2 cloves garlic, minced
- 4 cups vegetable broth
- 1 teaspoon dried thyme

- 1/2 teaspoon paprika
- Salt and pepper to taste
- Fresh parsley for garnish

**Instructions:**

1. Heat olive oil in a large pot over medium heat. Add the chopped onion and sauté until translucent.
2. Stir in the carrots, parsnips, sweet potato, and garlic and cook for an additional 5 minutes.
3. Add the vegetable broth, thyme, paprika, salt, and pepper. Bring to a boil.
4. Reduce heat to low, cover, and simmer for about 20-30 minutes or until the vegetables are tender.
5. Use an immersion blender to puree the soup until smooth (or leave it chunky based on your preference).
6. Adjust seasoning as necessary and serve hot, garnished with fresh parsley.

## 4. Spiced Apple Crumble

**Ingredients:**

- **For the fruit filling:**
- 4 cups apples, peeled and sliced (Granny Smith or Honeycrisp)
- 1/2 cup brown sugar
- 1 tablespoon lemon juice
- 1 teaspoon cinnamon
- 1/2 teaspoon nutmeg
- **For the crumble topping:**
- 1 cup rolled oats

- 1 cup all-purpose flour
- 1/2 cup brown sugar
- 1/2 teaspoon cinnamon
- 1/2 cup cold butter, cubed
- Pinch of salt

**Instructions:**

1. **Preheat the oven** to 350°F (175°C).
2. In a large bowl, mix sliced apples, brown sugar, lemon juice, cinnamon, and nutmeg. Spread the mixture in a greased baking dish.
3. In another bowl, combine oats, flour, brown sugar, cinnamon, and salt. Cut in the cold butter until the mixture resembles coarse crumbs.
4. Sprinkle the crumble topping evenly over the apple mixture.
5. Bake for 30-35 minutes or until the topping is golden and the apples are bubbling.
6. Serve warm with ice cream or whipped cream if desired.

These recipes embody warmth, tradition, and the spirit of the season, perfect for celebrating Yule with family and friends! Enjoy your festive feast!

# Imbolc (February 1 - 2)

**Significance:** Imbolc is a time of light and purification, honoring Brigid, the goddess of fire and fertility. It marks the halfway point between winter and spring.

### 1. Brigid's Bread (Soda Bread)

**Ingredients:**

- 4 cups all-purpose flour
- 1 teaspoon baking soda
- 1 teaspoon salt
- 1 3/4 cups buttermilk
- Optional: 1/4 cup honey or sugar for sweetness

**Instructions:**

1. Preheat your oven to 425°F (220°C). Grease a baking sheet or line it with parchment paper.
2. In a large bowl, mix the flour, baking soda, and salt together.
3. Create a well in the center and gradually add the buttermilk, mixing until a soft dough forms. Optionally, fold in honey for sweetness.
4. Turn the dough out onto a floured surface and knead gently for about 1-2 minutes until smooth.
5. Shape the dough into a round loaf and place it on the baking sheet. Score a deep cross on top with a knife.

6. Bake for 30-40 minutes or until the bread is golden brown and sounds hollow when tapped on the bottom.
7. Let it cool slightly before slicing. Serve with butter or preserves.

## 2. Herbed Vegetable Soup

**Ingredients:**
- 2 tablespoons olive oil
- 1 onion, chopped
- 2 cloves garlic, minced
- 3 carrots, sliced
- 3 stalks celery, chopped
- 4 cups vegetable broth
- 2 cups potatoes, diced
- 1 teaspoon dried thyme
- 1 teaspoon dried rosemary
- Salt and pepper to taste
- Fresh parsley for garnish

**Instructions:**
1. In a large pot, heat the olive oil over medium heat. Add the onion and garlic, cooking until softened.
2. Stir in the carrots and celery, cooking for another 5-7 minutes.
3. Add the vegetable broth and potatoes, then bring to a boil.
4. Reduce heat and stir in thyme and rosemary. Season with salt and pepper.
5. Simmer for 20-30 minutes until the vegetables are

tender.

6. Serve garnished with fresh parsley.

## 3. Candlemas Cake (Spiced Almond Cake)

**Ingredients:**
- 1 cup almond flour
- 1 cup all-purpose flour
- 1 teaspoon baking powder
- 1/2 teaspoon baking soda
- 1 teaspoon cinnamon
- 1/2 teaspoon nutmeg
- 1/4 teaspoon salt
- 1/2 cup butter, softened
- 1 cup sugar
- 3 large eggs
- 1 cup milk
- 1 teaspoon vanilla extract
- Optional: sliced almonds for topping

**Instructions:**
1. Preheat the oven to 350°F (175°C) and grease a cake pan.
2. In a bowl, whisk together the almond flour, all-purpose flour, baking powder, baking soda, spices, and salt.
3. In another bowl, cream the butter and sugar until light and fluffy. Add eggs, one at a time, mixing well after each.
4. Add milk and vanilla extract; mix well.
5. Gradually add the dry ingredients to the wet mixture,

stirring until just combined.

6. Pour the batter into the prepared cake pan and sprinkle sliced almonds on top, if desired.
7. Bake for 30-40 minutes or until a toothpick comes out clean. Let it cool before serving.

## *4. Apple and Honey Glazed Roasted Root Vegetables*

**Ingredients:**

- 4 cups assorted root vegetables (carrots, parsnips, potatoes)
- 2 tablespoons olive oil
- 2 tablespoons honey
- 2 teaspoons dried thyme
- Salt and pepper to taste
- Fresh apple slices for garnish

**Instructions:**

1. Preheat the oven to 400°F (200°C).
2. Peel and chop the root vegetables into bite-sized pieces.
3. In a large bowl, combine olive oil, honey, thyme, salt, and pepper.
4. Add the vegetables to the bowl and toss to coat evenly.
5. Spread the vegetables on a baking sheet in a single layer.
6. Roast for 30-35 minutes, flipping halfway through, until they are golden and tender.
7. Serve garnished with fresh apple slices.

## *5. Imbolc Herbal Tea*

**Ingredients:**
- 1 tablespoon dried chamomile flowers
- 1 tablespoon dried peppermint leaves
- 1 tablespoon dried rose hips
- 1 tablespoon dried lemon balm
- Honey or lemon (optional)

**Instructions:**
1. In a bowl, mix all the dried herbs together.
2. Boil water in a teapot or pot.
3. Place 1-2 teaspoons of the herbal mixture into a teabag or tea infuser.
4. Pour hot water over the herbs and let steep for about 5-10 minutes.
5. Strain and serve hot, adding honey or lemon to taste.

## 6. Recipe: Creamy Potato and Leek Soup

**Ingredients:**
- 3 leeks, washed and sliced
- 4 large potatoes, peeled and chopped
- 1 onion, diced
- 4 cups vegetable broth
- 1 cup heavy cream or coconut milk
- 2 tablespoons olive oil
- Salt and pepper to taste
- Fresh chives for garnish

**Instructions:**

1. In a pot, heat olive oil and sauté the leeks and onion until translucent.
2. Add the potatoes and broth, bringing to a boil. Reduce heat and simmer until potatoes are tender.
3. Blend the soup until smooth, then stir in the cream or coconut milk. Season with salt and pepper.
4. Serve hot, garnished with fresh chives.

# Ostara (Spring Equinox - March 21)

**Significance:** Ostara celebrates the spring equinox, symbolizing rebirth, fertility, and the return of life to the earth.

### 1. Spring Vegetable Quiche

**Ingredients:**

- 1 pie crust (store-bought or homemade)
- 4 large eggs
- 1 cup milk (or plant-based alternative)
- 1 cup chopped asparagus
- 1 cup baby spinach
- 1/2 cup chopped green onions
- 1 cup shredded cheese (cheddar, goat, or your choice)
- Salt and pepper to taste

**Instructions:**

1. Preheat the oven to 375°F (190°C).
2. Roll out the pie crust and fit it into a 9-inch pie dish. Trim excess dough and poke the bottom with a fork.
3. In a skillet, lightly sauté the asparagus for about 3 minutes. Add the spinach and green onions to wilt them.
4. In a large bowl, whisk together the eggs and milk. Season with salt and pepper.
5. Spread the sautéed vegetables evenly over the crust,

then sprinkle the cheese on top.
6. Pour the egg mixture over the vegetables and cheese.
7. Bake for 30-35 minutes, or until the quiche is set and golden. Let it cool for a few minutes before slicing.

## *2. Honey and Lavender Lemonade*

**Ingredients:**
- 1 cup fresh lemon juice (about 4-6 lemons)
- 1/2 cup honey (or to taste)
- 4 cups water
- 2 tablespoons dried culinary lavender
- Lemon slices (for garnish)
- Fresh lavender sprigs (for garnish)

**Instructions:**
1. In a saucepan, combine 1 cup of water, honey, and dried lavender. Bring to a simmer over medium heat, stirring until the honey dissolves.
2. Remove from heat and let steep for about 15 minutes. Strain out the lavender and let the syrup cool.
3. In a pitcher, combine the lemon juice and the lavender syrup. Add the remaining 3 cups of water and stir well.
4. Chill in the refrigerator for at least an hour before serving. Serve over ice, garnished with lemon slices and fresh lavender.

## *3. Herbal Pasta Salad*

**Ingredients:**
- 12 ounces pasta (penne or fusilli)

- 1 cup cherry tomatoes, halved
- 1 cup cucumber, diced
- 1/2 cup red onion, thinly sliced
- 1/4 cup fresh parsley, chopped
- 1/4 cup fresh basil, chopped
- 1/4 cup olive oil
- 2 tablespoons balsamic vinegar
- Salt and pepper to taste

**Instructions:**

1. Cook the pasta according to package instructions. Drain and rinse under cold water to cool.
2. In a large bowl, combine the cooled pasta, cherry tomatoes, cucumber, red onion, parsley, and basil.
3. In a small bowl, whisk together the olive oil, balsamic vinegar, salt, and pepper. Pour over the pasta salad and toss to coat.
4. Refrigerate for 30 minutes before serving to let the flavors meld.

## *4. Rainbow Fruit Salad*

**Ingredients:**

- 1 cup strawberries, hulled and quartered
- 1 cup orange segments
- 1 cup pineapple, diced
- 1 cup green grapes, halved
- 1 cup blueberries
- Juice of 1 lime
- 1 tablespoon honey (optional)

- Fresh mint (for garnish)

**Instructions:**

1. In a large bowl, combine all the fruit.
2. In a separate small bowl, whisk together the lime juice and honey (if using).
3. Drizzle the lime mixture over the fruit and toss gently to combine.
4. Garnish with fresh mint before serving.

## 5. Ostara Egg Cookies

**Ingredients:**

- 2 cups all-purpose flour
- 1/2 teaspoon baking powder
- 1/4 teaspoon salt
- 1/2 cup unsalted butter, softened
- 1 cup sugar
- 1 large egg
- 1 teaspoon vanilla extract
- 1 teaspoon almond extract
- Food coloring (optional)
- Royal icing for decorating

**Instructions:**

1. Preheat the oven to 350°F (175°C). Line a baking sheet with parchment paper.
2. In a bowl, whisk together the flour, baking powder, and salt.
3. In another bowl, cream together the softened butter and sugar until light and fluffy. Beat in the egg, vanilla,

and almond extracts.
4. Gradually add the dry ingredients to the wet ingredients, mixing until combined.
5. Roll out the dough on a floured surface to about 1/4 inch thick. Cut out egg shapes using a cookie cutter.
6. Place the cookies on the prepared baking sheet and bake for 8-10 minutes or until the edges are lightly golden.
7. Let cool completely before decorating with royal icing or using food coloring to create vibrant designs.

## 6. Recipe: Spring Vegetable Quiche

**Ingredients:**
- 1 pre-made pie crust
- 1 cup broccoli florets
- 1 cup asparagus, trimmed and chopped
- 1/2 cup spinach
- 4 large eggs
- 1 cup milk
- 1 cup shredded cheese (cheddar or feta)
- Salt and pepper to taste

**Instructions:**
1. Preheat the oven to 375°F (190°C).
2. In a skillet, lightly sauté broccoli, asparagus, and spinach until tender.
3. In a bowl, whisk together eggs, milk, salt, and pepper. Stir in the vegetables and cheese.
4. Pour the mixture into the pie crust and bake for 35-40 minutes until set.

5. Allow to cool slightly before slicing. Serve warm or at room temperature.

# Beltane (May 1)

**Significance:** Beltane marks the arrival of summer and is a festival of fertility, fire, and fun.

### 1. Elderflower Cordial

A refreshing drink to toast the season.

**Ingredients:**

- 15-20 elderflower heads (ensure they are pesticide-free)
- 1 liter of water
- 500g granulated sugar
- Juice of 2 lemons
- 1 tsp citric acid (optional)

**Instructions:**

1. Rinse the elderflower heads gently to remove any insects.
2. In a large pot, bring the water to a boil. Remove from heat and add the elderflowers, sugar, lemon juice, and citric acid.
3. Stir until the sugar has dissolved. Cover and let it steep for 24 hours in a cool place.
4. Strain the mixture through a fine sieve or cheesecloth into a clean bottle.
5. Store in the fridge and dilute with water or sparkling

water when serving.

## 2. Wildflower Salad

A colorful, edible flower salad symbolizing fertility and growth.

**Ingredients:**

- 4 cups mixed salad greens (like arugula, spinach, or lettuce)
- 1 cup edible flowers (e.g., violets, nasturtiums, dandelions, or calendula)
- 1 cucumber, sliced
- 1 cup cherry tomatoes, halved
- 1/2 cup goat cheese, crumbled (optional)
- 1/4 cup olive oil
- 2 tbsp balsamic vinegar
- Salt and pepper to taste

**Instructions:**

1. In a large bowl, combine salad greens, edible flowers, cucumber, and cherry tomatoes.
2. In a small mixing bowl, whisk together olive oil, balsamic vinegar, salt, and pepper.
3. Drizzle the dressing over the salad and toss gently to combine.
4. Top with crumbled goat cheese if desired. Serve immediately.

## 3. Honey and Herb Glazed Carrots

A simple, sweet dish to celebrate the earth's bounty.

**Ingredients:**
- 500g baby carrots (or sliced regular carrots)
- 2 tbsp honey
- 1 tbsp olive oil
- 1 tsp dried thyme (or 1 tbsp fresh thyme)
- Salt and pepper to taste

**Instructions:**
1. Preheat your oven to 200°C (400°F).
2. In a large bowl, mix honey, olive oil, thyme, salt, and pepper.
3. Add the carrots to the bowl and toss them in the honey mixture until well coated.
4. Spread the carrots on a baking sheet in a single layer.
5. Roast for 20-25 minutes, or until tender and slightly caramelized, stirring halfway through. Serve warm.

## 4. Maypole Cake

A delightful cake decorated with flowers to symbolize the Maypole tradition.

**Ingredients:**
- 250g unsalted butter, softened
- 250g granulated sugar
- 4 large eggs
- 250g all-purpose flour
- 2 tsp baking powder
- 1/2 tsp salt
- 100ml milk
- Edible flowers for decoration (e.g., pansies, violets)

- Buttercream frosting (homemade or store-bought)

**Instructions:**
1. Preheat your oven to 180°C (350°F). Grease and flour two 8-inch round cake pans.
2. In a mixing bowl, beat the butter and sugar until light and fluffy.
3. Add eggs, one at a time, mixing well after each addition.
4. In another bowl, whisk together flour, baking powder, and salt.
5. Gradually add the dry ingredients to the wet mixture, alternating with milk, mixing until smooth.
6. Divide the batter between the prepared pans and bake for 25-30 minutes or until a toothpick comes out clean.
7. Once cooled, frost with buttercream and decorate with edible flowers to create a Maypole effect.

## *5. Floral Herbal Tea*

A soothing beverage to enjoy during the festivities.

**Ingredients:**
- 1 tbsp dried chamomile flowers
- 1 tbsp dried hibiscus flowers
- 1 tbsp dried rose petals
- 1 tsp dried mint leaves
- 4 cups boiling water
- Honey or sugar to taste (optional)

**Instructions:**
1. In a teapot, combine chamomile, hibiscus, rose petals, and mint.

2. Pour boiling water over the flowers and leave to steep for 5-10 minutes depending on your desired strength.
3. Strain the tea into cups and sweeten with honey or sugar if desired.
4. Serve hot or chilled, garnished with a fresh mint sprig or a few edible flowers if available.

## *6. Recipe: Honey and Elderflower Fizz*

**Ingredients:**
- 1 cup elderflower cordial
- 1 bottle sparkling water or champagne
- Fresh mint leaves
- Lemon slices
- Ice cubes

**Instructions:**
1. In a tall glass, combine elderflower cordial with a splash of sparkling water/champagne.
2. Add ice cubes, mint leaves, and a lemon slice for garnish.
3. Stir gently and serve in a celebratory manner, raising your glass to the summer.

# Litha (Summer Solstice - June 21)

**Significance:** Litha is a celebration of the summer solstice, the longest day of the year, filled with the abundance of life and energy.

### 1. Sun-Infused Herbal Tea

**Ingredients:**

- 4 cups water
- 1 cup fresh mint leaves (or 2 tablespoons dried mint)
- 1 cup fresh chamomile flowers (or 2 tablespoons dried chamomile)
- Honey or agave syrup (to taste)
- Lemon slices (for garnish)

**Instructions:**

1. Boil 4 cups of water and allow it to cool slightly.
2. In a large glass jar, combine fresh mint and chamomile.
3. Pour the warm water over the herbs, cover the jar with a lid or plastic wrap, and place it in direct sunlight for 2-4 hours.
4. After infusing, strain the tea into a pitcher. Sweeten with honey or agave syrup to taste.
5. Serve chilled over ice, garnished with lemon slices.

### 2. Grilled Vegetable Skewers

**Ingredients:**
- 1 zucchini, sliced
- 1 bell pepper, cubed
- 1 red onion, cubed
- 2 cups cherry tomatoes
- 1 cup mushrooms, halved
- 1/4 cup olive oil
- Salt and pepper (to taste)
- Fresh herbs (like thyme or rosemary)

**Instructions:**
1. Preheat your grill to medium heat.
2. In a bowl, combine all the chopped vegetables. Drizzle with olive oil and season with salt, pepper, and fresh herbs. Toss to coat.
3. Thread the vegetables onto skewers, alternating types for color.
4. Place the skewers on the grill and cook for about 10-15 minutes, turning occasionally, until the vegetables are tender and slightly charred.
5. Serve warm with a side of dipping sauce or as a side dish.

## *3. Berry Pavlova*

**Ingredients:**
- 4 egg whites
- 1 cup granulated sugar
- 1 teaspoon vanilla extract

- 1 teaspoon white vinegar
- 2 cups mixed berries (strawberries, blueberries, raspberries)
- 1 cup heavy whipping cream
- 2 tablespoons powdered sugar
- Fresh mint leaves (for garnish)

**Instructions:**

1. Preheat the oven to 300°F (150°C) and line a baking sheet with parchment paper.
2. In a large bowl, beat the egg whites until stiff peaks form.
3. Gradually add the granulated sugar, beating well after each addition. Stir in the vanilla and vinegar.
4. Spoon the meringue onto the prepared baking sheet, shaping it into a nest with a slight dip in the center.
5. Bake for 1 hour, then turn off the oven and let the meringue cool completely.
6. Whip the cream with powdered sugar until soft peaks form. Spread over the cooled meringue and top with fresh berries.
7. Garnish with mint leaves before serving.

## 4. Summer Solstice Salad

**Ingredients:**

- 4 cups mixed greens (arugula, spinach, or lettuce)
- 1 cup sliced strawberries
- 1 cup cucumber, sliced
- 1/2 cup feta cheese, crumbled
- 1/4 cup walnuts or pecans, toasted

- 1/4 cup balsamic vinaigrette

**Instructions:**

1. In a large bowl, combine the mixed greens, strawberries, cucumber, feta cheese, and nuts.
2. Drizzle with balsamic vinaigrette and toss gently to combine.
3. Serve immediately, garnished with extra strawberries or nuts if desired.

## *5. Honey & Lavender Lemonade*

**Ingredients:**

- 1 cup fresh lemon juice (about 4-6 lemons)
- 1/2 cup honey (or more to taste)
- 4 cups water
- 2 tablespoons dried culinary lavender
- Lemon slices and lavender sprigs (for garnish)

**Instructions:**

1. In a small saucepan, combine 1 cup of water and dried lavender. Bring to a simmer over low heat and let it steep for about 10 minutes. Strain the lavender and discard the flowers.
2. In a large pitcher, combine the lemon juice, honey, and the lavender-infused water. Stir well until the honey is dissolved.
3. Add the remaining 3 cups of water and adjust sweetness if needed.
4. Chill in the refrigerator and serve over ice, garnished with lemon slices and lavender sprigs.

These recipes reflect the abundance and vibrancy of summer,

making them perfect for celebrating Litha. Enjoy the seasonal flavors and the joy of gathering with loved ones!

## 6. Recipe: Grilled Summer Vegetable Salad

**Ingredients:**
- 2 zucchini, sliced
- 1 eggplant, diced
- 1 red bell pepper, sliced
- 1 yellow bell pepper, sliced
- 2 tablespoons olive oil
- Salt and pepper
- Fresh basil for garnish
- Balsamic glaze (for drizzling)

**Instructions:**
1. Preheat the grill to medium heat.
2. Toss the vegetables with olive oil, salt, and pepper.
3. Grill for 5-7 minutes per side or until tender and slightly charred.
4. Arrange on a platter, drizzle with balsamic glaze, and garnish with fresh basil. Serve warm or at room temperature.

# Lammas (August 1)

**Significance:** Lammas celebrates the first harvest, particularly of grain. It's a time for gratitude and abundance.

## 1. Fresh Cornbread

**Ingredients:**

- 1 cup cornmeal
- 1 cup all-purpose flour
- 2 tablespoons sugar
- 1 tablespoon baking powder
- ½ teaspoon salt
- 1 cup buttermilk
- 2 large eggs
- ½ cup melted butter
- 1 cup fresh corn kernels (or canned/frozen if needed)

**Instructions:**

1. Preheat your oven to 400°F (200°C). Grease an 8-inch square baking dish or a cast-iron skillet.
2. In a large bowl, mix the cornmeal, flour, sugar, baking powder, and salt.
3. In another bowl, whisk together the buttermilk, eggs, and melted butter.
4. Pour the wet ingredients into the dry ingredients,

stirring until just combined. Fold in the corn kernels.

5. Pour the batter into the prepared baking dish and smooth the top.
6. Bake for 20-25 minutes, or until golden brown and a toothpick inserted in the center comes out clean.
7. Allow to cool slightly before serving. Enjoy with honey or butter.

## *2. Herbed Wheat Berry Salad*

**Ingredients:**
- 1 cup wheat berries
- 4 cups water
- 1 cup cherry tomatoes, halved
- ½ cucumber, diced
- 1 bell pepper, diced
- ¼ cup red onion, finely chopped
- ½ cup fresh parsley, chopped
- ¼ cup olive oil
- 2 tablespoons lemon juice
- Salt and pepper to taste

**Instructions:**
1. Rinse the wheat berries under cold water. In a pot, combine wheat berries and water. Bring to a boil, then reduce heat and simmer for about 40-60 minutes until tender.
2. Drain and rinse the wheat berries under cold water. Set aside to cool.
3. In a large bowl, combine the cooked wheat berries, cherry tomatoes, cucumber, bell pepper, red onion, and

parsley.

4. In a small bowl, whisk together the olive oil, lemon juice, salt, and pepper.
5. Pour the dressing over the salad and toss to combine. Serve chilled or at room temperature.

## *3. Honey Oat Bread*

**Ingredients:**
- 2 cups whole wheat flour
- 1 cup rolled oats
- 1 packet (2 ¼ tsp) active dry yeast
- 1 ½ cups warm water (110°F/45°C)
- ¼ cup honey
- 2 tablespoons olive oil
- 1 teaspoon salt

**Instructions:**
1. In a large mixing bowl, combine warm water, honey, and yeast. Let sit for 5-10 minutes until frothy.
2. Stir in olive oil and salt.
3. Gradually add whole wheat flour and oats, mixing until a dough forms.
4. Knead the dough for 8-10 minutes until smooth. Place in a greased bowl, cover with a cloth, and let rise in a warm spot for about 1 hour, or until doubled in size.
5. Preheat your oven to 375°F (190°C).
6. Punch down the dough and shape it into a loaf. Place it in a greased loaf pan.
7. Let it rise for another 30 minutes. Bake for 30-35 minutes until golden brown and sounds hollow when

tapped.

8. Cool on a wire rack before slicing.

## 4. Apple and Cinnamon Galette

**Ingredients:**

- 1 pre-made pie crust (or homemade)
- 3-4 apples, peeled and sliced
- ¼ cup sugar
- 1 tablespoon lemon juice
- 1 teaspoon cinnamon
- 1 tablespoon flour for filling
- 1 egg (for egg wash)
- Additional sugar for sprinkling

**Instructions:**

1. Preheat your oven to 375°F (190°C).
2. In a bowl, combine the sliced apples, sugar, lemon juice, cinnamon, and flour. Toss until well coated.
3. Roll out the pie crust on a baking sheet lined with parchment paper.
4. Mound the apple mixture in the center of the crust, leaving about a 1.5-inch border.
5. Fold the edges of the crust over the filling, pleating it as you go.
6. Beat the egg and brush it over the crust. Sprinkle the edges with sugar.
7. Bake for 30-35 minutes until the apples are tender and the crust is golden.
8. Serve warm, optionally topped with vanilla ice cream.

## 5. Zucchini and Herb Fritters

**Ingredients:**
- 2 medium zucchinis, grated
- 1 cup all-purpose flour
- 2 large eggs
- ¼ cup grated Parmesan cheese
- ¼ cup fresh herbs (like parsley, basil, or dill), chopped
- 1 teaspoon garlic powder
- Salt and pepper to taste
- Olive oil for frying

**Instructions:**
1. Place the grated zucchini in a clean kitchen towel and squeeze out excess moisture.
2. In a large bowl, combine the zucchini, flour, eggs, Parmesan, herbs, garlic powder, salt, and pepper. Mix until combined.
3. Heat a large skillet over medium heat and add a thin layer of olive oil.
4. Drop spoonfuls of the zucchini mixture into the hot skillet, flattening them slightly with the back of the spoon.
5. Fry for 3-4 minutes on each side until golden and crispy.
6. Drain on paper towels and serve warm, possibly with a yogurt dip or sauce.

## 6. Recipe: Rustic Bread with Honey Butter

**Ingredients:**
- **For the bread:**
- 3 cups all-purpose flour
- 1 packet (2¼ teaspoons) active dry yeast
- 1 cup warm water
- 1 tablespoon sugar
- 1 tablespoon salt
- 2 tablespoons olive oil
- **For the honey butter:**
- 1/2 cup unsalted butter, softened
- 1/4 cup honey
- A sprinkle of sea salt

**Instructions:**
1. Combine warm water, yeast, and sugar and let sit until frothy (about 5 minutes).
2. In a large bowl, mix flour and salt. Add the yeast mixture and olive oil, kneading until smooth.
3. Let the dough rise until doubled in size (about 1 hour). Shape into a loaf and let rise again for 30 minutes. Preheat oven to 375°F (190°C).
4. Bake the bread for 25-30 minutes until golden brown.
5. Meanwhile, mix softened butter with honey and sea salt. Serve the bread warm with honey butter.

# Mabon (Autumn Equinox - September 21)

**Significance:** Mabon is a time of thanksgiving and reflection as daylight diminishes. It is a moment to take stock of the harvest and prepare for the coming winter.

### 1. Roasted Root Vegetable Medley

**Ingredients:**

- 2 medium carrots, chopped
- 1 medium parsnip, chopped
- 1 medium sweet potato, cubed
- 1 red onion, cut into wedges
- 4 cloves garlic, whole
- 3 tablespoons olive oil
- 1 teaspoon dried thyme
- Salt and pepper to taste
- Fresh parsley for garnish (optional)

**Instructions:**

1. Preheat your oven to 425°F (220°C).
2. In a large bowl, combine the carrots, parsnip, sweet potato, red onion, and garlic.
3. Drizzle with olive oil, then sprinkle with thyme, salt,

and pepper. Toss until vegetables are evenly coated.

4. Spread the mixture on a baking sheet in a single layer.
5. Roast in the oven for 25–30 minutes, stirring halfway through, until the vegetables are tender and caramelized.
6. Remove from oven, garnish with fresh parsley if desired, and serve warm.

## *2. Apple Crisp*

**Ingredients:**
- 5 medium apples, peeled, cored, and sliced
- 1 tablespoon lemon juice
- 1 teaspoon ground cinnamon
- 1 cup rolled oats
- 1 cup brown sugar
- 1/2 cup all-purpose flour
- 1/2 cup unsalted butter, softened
- 1/2 teaspoon salt

**Instructions:**
1. Preheat the oven to 350°F (175°C).
2. In a large bowl, toss the sliced apples with lemon juice and cinnamon. Transfer to a greased 9x13 inch baking dish.
3. In another bowl, combine oats, brown sugar, flour, softened butter, and salt. Mix until crumbly.
4. Spread the oat mixture evenly over the apples in the baking dish.
5. Bake for 30–35 minutes, until the topping is golden brown and the apples are bubbly.

6. Let cool slightly before serving. Enjoy warm, optionally with vanilla ice cream.

### *3. Pumpkin Soup*

**Ingredients:**
- 2 tablespoons olive oil
- 1 medium onion, diced
- 3 cloves garlic, minced
- 1 medium carrot, diced
- 1 medium potato, peeled and diced
- 4 cups pumpkin puree (canned or fresh)
- 4 cups vegetable or chicken broth
- 1 teaspoon ground nutmeg
- 1 teaspoon ground cinnamon
- Salt and pepper to taste
- 1 cup coconut milk (optional)
- Pumpkin seeds for garnish

**Instructions:**
1. In a large pot, heat olive oil over medium heat. Add onion and garlic, sautéing until fragrant and translucent.
2. Add the carrot and potato, cooking for about 5 minutes until softened.
3. Stir in the pumpkin puree, broth, nutmeg, cinnamon, salt, and pepper. Bring to a boil, then reduce the heat and simmer for about 20 minutes.
4. For a creamy texture, blend the soup using an immersion blender or in batches in a regular blender.

5. Stir in coconut milk if desired, then taste and adjust seasonings.
6. Serve hot, garnished with pumpkin seeds.

## *4. Stuffed Acorn Squash*

**Ingredients:**

- 2 acorn squash, halved and seeds removed
- 1 cup quinoa or wild rice, cooked
- 1 cup cooked black beans (canned or homemade)
- 1/2 cup corn (fresh or frozen)
- 1/2 teaspoon cumin
- 1 teaspoon chili powder
- Salt and pepper to taste
- 1/2 cup shredded cheese (optional)
- Fresh cilantro for garnish

**Instructions:**

1. Preheat your oven to 400°F (200°C).
2. Place acorn squash halves cut-side down on a baking sheet and roast for 20–25 minutes until tender.
3. While the squash is roasting, in a large bowl, combine the cooked quinoa or rice, black beans, corn, cumin, chili powder, salt, and pepper.
4. Once the squash is done, carefully flip them cut-side up and fill each half with the quinoa mixture, pressing down gently.
5. If using cheese, sprinkle on top and return to the oven for an additional 10 minutes.
6. Remove from the oven, garnish with fresh cilantro, and serve warm.

## 5. Spiced Cider

**Ingredients:**

- 1 gallon apple cider
- 1 orange, sliced
- 4 whole cloves
- 4 cinnamon sticks
- 1 star anise (optional)
- 1/4 teaspoon ground nutmeg
- Honey or maple syrup to taste (optional)

**Instructions:**

1. In a large pot, combine apple cider, orange slices, cloves, cinnamon sticks, star anise, and nutmeg.
2. Heat over medium heat until simmering, then reduce heat to low and let it steep for at least 30 minutes.
3. Taste and add honey or maple syrup if you prefer a sweeter cider.
4. Strain out the spices and orange before serving.
5. Serve hot in mugs, garnished with a cinnamon stick or orange slice if desired.

## 6. Recipe: Harvest Fruit Crisp

**Ingredients:**

- 4 cups mixed fruit (apples, pears, and berries)
- 1 tablespoon lemon juice
- 1 cup rolled oats
- 1 cup brown sugar

- 1 cup all-purpose flour
- 1 teaspoon cinnamon
- 1/2 cup cold butter, diced

**Instructions:**

1. Preheat the oven to 350°F (175°C).
2. In a bowl, toss the mixed fruit with lemon juice and place in a greased baking dish.
3. In another bowl, combine oats, brown sugar, flour, cinnamon, and diced butter. Mix until crumbly.
4. Sprinkle the oat mixture over the fruit and bake for 30-35 minutes until bubbly and golden brown.
5. Serve warm with vanilla ice cream or whipped cream.

Celebrating the Sabbats as a cottage witch is about nourishing the soul and feeding the spirit. These recipes not only sustain the body but also create an atmosphere of warmth, love, and gratitude within your home. Gather friends and family, create a beautiful space, and let the magic of the seasons inspire you to celebrate the cycles of life.

Each Sabbat is a unique opportunity to weave nature into your practice, honor your ancestors, and embrace the powerful energies of the earth. May your kitchens always be filled with the fragrant aromas of the seasons, and may your heart be open to the joys of the earth and its gifts!

# Chapter 22: Magical Correspondences

∞∞∞

Understanding magical correspondences is a vital element that weaves together the natural world with the mystical. Here we will explore the intricate relationships between herbs, crystals, essential oils, planets, the Wheel of the Year, and zodiac signs. By learning and utilizing these correspondences, the cottage witch can enhance their magical workings, infuse everyday practices with intention, and align themselves more closely with the rhythms of nature and the cosmos.

## *Colors*

**1. Gold**

- **Associations**: Wealth, prosperity, success, solar energy, abundance, illumination
- **Uses**: Attracting prosperity, enhancing self-confidence, promoting success in endeavors, solar magic, manifestation rituals.

**2. Silver**

- **Associations**: Intuition, emotional balance, lunar energy, reflection, purity, the feminine divine
- **Uses**: Enhancing intuition, promoting emotional healing, strengthening psychic abilities, rituals related to the moon, protection.

3. **Red**
    - **Associations**: Passion, love, strength, courage, vitality
    - **Uses**: Enhancing love and relationships, boosting energy, courage in difficult situations, protection spells.

4. **Blue**
    - **Associations**: Calm, wisdom, truth, communication, healing
    - **Uses**: Promoting peace and tranquility, enhancing communication, tapping into wisdom, healing rituals.

5. **Green**
    - **Associations**: Growth, fertility, abundance, nature, health
    - **Uses**: Attracting prosperity, growth in ventures, health, connecting with nature, fertility spells.

6. **Yellow**
    - **Associations**: Joy, intellect, clarity, confidence, creativity
    - **Uses**: Promoting happiness, encouraging creativity, boosting confidence, clarity of thought, decision-making spells.

7. **Purple**
    - **Associations**: Spirituality, intuition, ambition, magic, royalty
    - **Uses**: Enhancing spiritual awareness, attracting ambition and success, connecting to higher realms, extending magical work.

8. **Black**
    - **Associations**: Protection, banishment, mystery, strength

- **Uses**: Protection spells, banishing negativity, deep meditation, working with shadows and the subconscious.

9. **White**
    - **Associations**: Purity, clarity, protection, peace, new beginnings
    - **Uses**: Blessings, purification rituals, drawing in peace, enhancing clarity, setting intentions.

10. **Orange**
    - **Associations**: Creativity, enthusiasm, joy, stimulation, attraction
    - **Uses**: Enhancing creativity, promoting enthusiasm, attracting joy and success, stimulating motivation.

11. **Brown**
    - **Associations**: Stability, grounding, earthiness, protection, nature
    - **Uses**: Grounding energies, connecting with nature, protection, stability in life situations.

12. **Pink**
    - **Associations**: Love, compassion, emotional healing, beauty
    - **Uses**: Attracting love, fostering self-love and compassion, emotional healing, beauty rituals.

13. **Turquoise**
    - **Associations**: Healing, protection, communication, emotional balance
    - **Uses**: Healing rituals, promoting effective communication, protection during travel.

14. **Gray**
    - **Associations**: Neutrality, balance, indecision, wisdom

- **Uses**: Achieving balance, working through indecision, wise judgement, seeking neutrality in conflicts.

**15. Violet**

- **Associations**: Spiritual growth, intuition, connection to spirit
- **Uses**: Enhancing meditation, deepening intuition, connecting with the higher self.

## *Crystals*

Crystals are powerful allies for the cottage witch, acting as conduits of energy that aid in focusing intention. Here are a few essential crystals and their magical properties:

- **Amethyst**: Enhances intuition, protects against psychic attacks, and promotes peace.
- **Clear Quartz**: A master healer, amplifying energy and intention.
- **Citrine**: Encourages prosperity, abundance, and success.
- **Rose Quartz**: The stone of love and compassion, ideal for emotional healing.
- **Obsidian**: A powerful protective stone that shields against negativity.

**Practical Application**

Integrate crystals into your magical practice by creating crystal grids, charging water, or holding them during meditation to focus your intentions. For instance, you might carry a piece of citrine in your wallet to attract financial abundance, or place rose quartz near your bed to foster loving energy in your space.

## *Essential Oils*

Essential oils are concentrated plant extracts that carry the essence of herbs and flowers. They can be used in healing, cleansing, and enhancing magical practices. Some key oils and their properties include:

- **Lavender Oil**: Promotes relaxation and peace, great for sleep.
- **Peppermint Oil**: Invigorating and energizing, allies well with focus and clarity.
- **Frankincense Oil**: Used in spiritual practices for purification and enhancement of meditation.
- **Rose Oil**: Associated with love, beauty, and emotional support.
- **Cedarwood Oil**: Provides grounding energy and is often employed for protection.

**Practical Application**

To utilize essential oils, consider incorporating them into your daily rituals through diffusing, anointing candles, or creating personal blends for rituals. For example, adding a few drops of lavender oil to a bath can enhance relaxation, while using peppermint oil can boost clarity during study or work sessions.

## *Herbs*

Herbs are some of the primary tools of the cottage witch. Each herb carries its unique energetic properties and intuitive applications. Here are some key herbs and their correspondences:

- **Rosemary**: Linked to purification and protection. Ideal for cleansing spaces and memory enhancement.
- **Sage**: Renowned for its ability to ward off negativity and protect sacred spaces.
- **Lavender**: Associated with tranquillity, healing, and sleep. Useful in relaxation rituals.
- **Chamomile**: Related to peace and healing, especially for anxiety and sleep disorders.
- **Basil**: Tied to abundance and love, often used in prosperity spells.
- **Thyme**: Symbolizes courage and strength, great for empowering rituals.

**Practical Application**

Incorporate herbs by creating herbal sachets, infusions, or oils that align with your intention. For example, a sachet of lavender and chamomile can aid in restful sleep, while a mix of rosemary and sage can cleanse a space before ritual work.

## *The Planets*

Each planet in our solar system vibrates with distinct energies that can enhance different aspects of magical workings:

- **Sun** (Leo): Symbolizes vitality, success, and leadership. Use during solar rituals for empowerment.
- **Moon** (Cancer): Represents intuition, emotions, and dreams. Ideal for reflection and feminine energy rituals.
- **Mars** (Aries): Embodies courage, strength, and action.

Suitable for spells on protection and assertiveness.
- **Mercury** (Gemini): Governs communication, intellect, and travel. Perfect for enhancing clarity in communication magic.
- **Venus** (Taurus/Libra): The planet of love, beauty, and harmony. Use during rituals focused on relationships and aesthetics.

**Practical Application**

Time your magical workings according to planetary hours and days. For instance, perform love spells on Fridays (Venus) or protective work on Tuesdays (Mars). Aligning your intentions with planetary influences amplifies their effectiveness.

## *The Wheel of the Year*

The Wheel of the Year marks the turning of the seasons and celebrates the rhythms of nature. Each sabbat has its energies and correspondences:

- **Samhain (October 31)**: A time to honor ancestors and deepen spiritual connection.
- **Yule (Winter Solstice)**: Celebrates rebirth and renewal; aligns with inner reflection.
- **Imbolc (February 1)**: Marks the beginning of spring; a time of purification and new beginnings.
- **Ostara (Spring Equinox)**: Represents fertility and growth; ideal for planting intentions.
- **Beltane (April 30)**: A celebration of love and passion, great for fertility and creative work.
- **Litha (Summer Solstice)**: A time of abundance and

strength; ideal for manifesting desires.

- **Lammas (August 1)**: Celebrates harvest and gratitude; a time for sharing and community.
- **Mabon (Autumn Equinox)**: A time of balance and thanksgiving, reflecting on the year's harvest.

**Practical Application**

Honor the Wheel of the Year through rituals that correspond with each sabbat. Create seasonal altars, perform relevant spells or celebrate with feasts that reflect the energies of each time. For instance, during Lammas, bake bread to give thanks for the harvest, or light a candle on Yule to celebrate the return of the light.

## *Zodiac Signs*

The zodiac can offer additional correspondences, aligning your personal energies with your magical practice. Each sign holds unique attributes and strengths:

- **Aries**: Courage, initiative, and dynamism. Ideal for spells of assertiveness.
- **Taurus**: Stability, comfort, and sensuality. Great for grounding rituals.
- **Gemini**: Communication, intellect, and adaptability. Use in expanding knowledge or promoting understanding.
- **Cancer**: Emotion, intuition, and nurturing. Useful for emotional healing.
- **Leo**: Confidence and creativity. Employ in leadership and artistic endeavors.

- **Virgo**: Practicality and organization. Best for grounding spells and detailed plans.
- **Libra**: Harmony and relationships. Enhance love and partnership rituals.
- **Scorpio**: Transformation and intensity. Use for deeper healing and shadow work.
- **Sagittarius**: Adventure and higher learning. Ideal for travel and exploration spells.
- **Capricorn**: Discipline and ambition. Assist in long-term goals and career endeavors.
- **Aquarius**: Innovation and social change. Useful for unique or unconventional ideas.
- **Pisces**: Intuition and spirituality. Align with dreamwork and emotional.

**Practical Application**

Cast your spells and create your intentions when the moon is in your sign or when the sun moves into a sign that resonates with your current goals. For instance, if you wish to work on self-esteem, focus on Leo energy when the sun is in Leo.

# Chapter 23: Your Path Forward

∞∞∞

Let's reflect on the path that has guided you to this moment. Now is the time to reflect on the lessons you've learned and integrate what you've learned into your life. Celebrate your personal growth and prepare for the next steps along your unique and magical path. Embracing the journey of a cottage witch is about more than just the spells and rituals; it's about the connection to nature, community, and self.

**The Journey of a Cottage Witch**

Cottage witchcraft invites you to step into a world where the mundane and the magical intertwine seamlessly, where the simple acts of everyday life are infused with intention and creativity. Each herb gathered from your garden, every candle lit on the altar, and each moment spent in contemplation of the moon is imbued with your energy and intention. This journey is about cultivating a sacred space, both outside in the physical realm and within your heart and mind.

Throughout this exploration, you have discovered the elements that resonate most with your spirit. Perhaps the earthy resonance of herbalism has awakened in you a desire to connect more deeply with the plants around you, or maybe the soothing rhythms of the seasons have inspired you to establish your own rituals honoring the turning of the wheel. Each of these practices brings you closer to the essence of cottage witchery—

embracing simplicity, authenticity, and the natural world.

### Reflecting on Personal Growth and Lessons Learned

Personal growth is an integral part of the cottage witch's journey. Each discovery, each practice, and even each challenge serves as a stepping stone toward a deeper understanding of yourself and your place in the universe. Reflect on the transformation you've undergone since you first ventured into this path. What hallowed moments stand out to you? Have you noticed shifts in your confidence, your intuition, or your connection to the natural world?

It's crucial to recognize that every stumble is not a failure but a valuable lesson. Perhaps there were spells that didn't manifest as intended or rituals that felt disconnected. Each experience —successful or not—teaches resilience and adaptability. In the quiet moments, listen to the wisdom of these lessons. Ask yourself: How have you grown in compassion, for yourself and for others? How has your understanding of balance and harmony developed?

By acknowledging your progress, you empower yourself to move forward boldly. Keep a journal of your reflections, noting down your thoughts and insights. This practice can help you track your evolution and serve as a source of inspiration in times of uncertainty.

### Encouragement to Continue Exploring, Learning, and Practicing

As you close this book, remember that the end of this journey is also the beginning of another. The art of cottage witchcraft is vast and ever-expanding, offering endless opportunities for exploration and discovery. Embrace your curiosity! Each season brings new energies, new plants, and new inspirations, waiting for your attentive heart to uncover them.

Engage in continuous learning—whether through books, workshops, online communities, or your own experiments. Seek out local plants and learn about their magical and medicinal properties. Attend seasonal festivals that celebrate the folk traditions of your ancestors, weaving those practices into your own unique tapestry of witchcraft. And never underestimate the value of collaborating and sharing experiences with fellow witches. The bonds formed in the community can enrich your practice immeasurably.

Make a commitment to practice regularly, allowing your craft to evolve as you grow. Set aside moments for grounding, for reflection, and for ritual. Whether it's a full moon ceremony or simply a few quiet minutes spent outdoors, these practices will serve as touchstones in your journey. Let your craft be flexible; it can change and adapt as you do.

Lastly, embody the tenets of patience and compassion in your practice. The journey of a cottage witch is not measured solely by the spells cast or the herbs harvested but rather by the spirit of love and gratitude that you infuse into each moment. Be gentle with yourself as you explore; growth can often happen in the quiet spaces between.

**Your Path Forward**

The path forward is a personal one, enriched by the uniqueness of your experiences, insights, and dreams. Picture it stretching out before you like an inviting forest glade, filled with opportunities and adventures awaiting your footsteps. You are empowered to weave your own magic, grounded in the wisdom of the past and propelled by your individuality.

As you step confidently into this chapter of your life, remind yourself that becoming a cottage witch is not a destination; it is a beautiful, ongoing process of evolution and connection. Embrace it with open arms, confident in the knowledge that you are a part of something greater. Trust the energies of the earth and the universe; they are your allies on this magnificent journey.

May your path shimmer with enchantment, your heart be filled with gratitude, and your spirit dance joyously amidst the blessings of the world. Welcome each dawn as a new beginning and allow the magic of your life to unfold in wondrous and unexpected ways. The tapestry of your journey is unique, and it is waiting to be woven anew, one thread of intention and love at a time.

Now, take a deep breath, savor this moment, and step forward into your magical future.

# Glossary

**Altar** - A sacred space used for rituals, offerings, and magical workings.

**Ancestor Work** - Practices honoring and communicating with ancestors for guidance and protection.

**Anointing** - The act of applying oil or herbs to an object or person for blessing or protection.

**Ashes** - The remnants of burnt offerings, often used in protection or cleansing spells.

**Beltane** - A festival marking the start of summer, celebrated with fertility and fire rituals.

**Bindings** - Spells intended to restrict or bind someone's actions or intentions.

**Blessing** - A prayer or ritual intended to bestow positive energy or protection upon someone or something.

**Calming Jar** - A jar filled with water and ingredients that symbolizes clarity and calmness.

**Candle Magic** - The use of candles to represent intentions during spellwork.

**Charm** - An object or spell designed to bring about a specific effect or intention.

**Cleansing** - The practice of purifying objects or spaces to remove negative energies.

**Cordial** - A herbal brew or tincture made for enjoyment or medicinal purposes.

**Cottage Witch** - A practitioner of witchcraft who focuses on home, nature, and everyday life.

**Crystal** - A mineral with specific energetic properties used in magic and healing.

**Divination** - The practice of seeking knowledge of the future or unknown through various methods.

**Dowsing** - A divination method using a forked stick or pendulum to locate water or energy sources.

**Elemental** - Referring to the four elements (earth, air, fire, water) commonly used in magic.

**Elemental Magick** - Magic that utilizes the energies of earth, air, fire, and water.

**Familiar** - A spirit or animal companion that aids a witch in magical workings.

**Focus** - The act of concentrating one's energy and intention on a specific goal during magical practices.

**Folk Magic** - Traditional magical practices rooted in cultural folklore and community knowledge.

**Grimoire** - A book of magical knowledge, spells, and rituals.

**Grounding** - A technique to connect oneself with the earth to achieve balance and focus.

**Harvest** - The gathering of crops, herbs, or energies, typically celebrated during the autumn equinox.

**Herb Bundle** - A collection of herbs tied together and used for protection or blessings.

**Herbalism** - The study and use of plants for medicinal or magical purposes.

**Intention** - The purpose or goal behind a magical working or spell.

**Invocations** - The act of calling upon spiritual entities or energies in rituals.

**Knot Magic** - The practice of tying knots to bind intentions into a spell.

**Meditation** - A practice to quiet the mind and connect with one's inner self or higher powers.

**Mirror Magic** - Using mirrors in spellwork to reflect energy or intentions.

**Moon phases** - The different stages of the moon which influence magical practices and rituals.

**Ostara** - A spring festival celebrating renewal and fertility, connected with the equinox.

**Pathworking** - A form of guided meditation that explores spiritual or magical realms.

**Pentacle** - A five-pointed star within a circle, often used as a symbol of protection and balance.

**Protection Spell** - A spell designed to guard against negative energies or influences.

**Proxy** - A representative used in spellwork, often involving someone else's energy or intention.

**Ritual** - A prescribed series of actions performed in a specific order for a spiritual purpose.

**Sabbats** - The eight seasonal festivals celebrated in Wicca and other pagan traditions.

**Sacred Space** - An area designated for spiritual practices, often cleansed and decorated for rituals.

**Scrying** - A divination practice involving gazing into a reflective surface to gain insights.

**Seasonal Rituals** - Ceremonies performed in accordance with seasonal changes or holidays.

**Sigil** - A symbol created for a specific magical purpose or intention.

**Spell Jar** - A container filled with herbs and items charged with the intention of a spell.

**Talisman** - An object believed to hold protective or magical properties.

**Veil** - The boundary between the physical and spiritual realms, often thinned during certain times.

**Waning Moon** - The phase of the moon where it decreases in visibility, often associated with banishing.

**Wildcrafting** - The practice of foraging for wild herbs and plants for magical or medicinal use.

**Witch's Ladder** - A charm made from knots that represent intentions, often used for wishes.

**Yule** - The winter festival celebrating the solstice and the return of the sun.

# Resources

**Books on Cottage Witchery:**

1. **"Cottage Witchery: Natural Magick for Hearth and Home" by** Ellen Dugan

Link: Amazon

2. **"The Green Witch: Your Complete Guide to the Natural Magic of Herbs, Flowers, Essential Oils, and More, " by** Arin Murphy-Hiscock

Link: Amazon

3. **"Grimoire for the Green Witch: A Complete Book of Shadows"** – Ann Moura

Link: Amazon

**Online Resources on Cottage Witchery:**

**The Herbal Academy**
- Link: Herbal Academy A place for learning about herbalism, which is integral to cottage witchery, with courses and resources.

**Pinterest - Cottage Witchery Boards**

- Link: Pinterest Cottage Witchery A platform with various pins dedicated to cottage witchcraft, home recipes, herbal remedies, and more.

**YouTube - Cottage Witchery Community**

- Link: YouTube Cottage Witchery A collection of videos from various creators discussing cottage witchery practices, DIY projects, and lifestyle tips.

# Bibliography

"A Modern Herbal" - Maud Grieve

"Botany for Gardeners" - Brian Capon

"Cottage Magic: The Spells to Awaken Your Inner Witch" - K. E. Rafferty

"Cottage Witch: The Simple Secrets to Enchant Your Home" - A. S. Patrick

"Earth Magic: Your Guide to Unlocking the Power of the Elemental Forces" - Serena Oak

"Gaia's Garden: A Guide to Home-Scale Permaculture" - Toby Hemenway

"Healing Herbs: A Beginner's Guide to Identifying, Foraging, and Using 50 Medicinal Plants" - Tina Sams

"Herb Magic for Beginners: How to Use Herbs to Create Magical Spells" - Ellen Dugan

"Herbal Magic: A Handbook of Natural Spells, Charms, and Potions" - Patricia Telesco

"Herbal Spellbook: 7 Magic Spells Using Herbs" - Nicole C. C. Baker

"Herbs for Enchantment: Recipes and Remedies" - Rowan O'Donnell

"Homegrown and Homemade a Guide to Nature Craft" - Kristine O'Rourke

"Magical Herbalism: The Secret Works of the Witch" - Scott Cunningham

"Natural Magic: The Great Healing Power of Herbs" - Mary-Gail M. Meandre

"Pagan Gardening: A Witch's Approach to Gardening" - L. Marie Bellew

"Plant Magic: The Secret to Making Magical Herbs" - T. M. Raine

"Rosemary Gladstar's Herbal Recipes for Vibrant Health" - Rosemary Gladstar

"The Complete Book of Herbal Remedies" - Gary Null

"The Complete Herbal Handbook for Farm and Stable" - Juliette de Bairacli Levy

"The Enchanted Garden: A Handbook of Herbs for Magical Charm" - Barbara A. Smith

"The Enchanted Herbal: A Practical Guide to Herbal Craft and Magic" - J. S. Smith

"The Garden of Herbal Delights" - Becca Williams

"The Garden Witch's Herbal: Green Magick, Herbalism, and Spirituality" - Amanda D. Smith

"The Garden Witch's Herbal: Green Magick, Herbalism, and Spirituality" - Amanda D. Smith

"The Green Witch's Guide to Herbs for Magical Uses" - Annabel de Vries

"The Herbal Apothecary: 100 Medicinal Herbs and How to Use Them" - JJ Pursell

"The Herbal Lore of Wise Women and Wortcunners: From the Stone Age to the Present" - Stephen Harrod Buhner

"The Herbal Medicine-Maker's Handbook: A Home Manual" - James Green

"The House Witch: Your Complete Guide to Creating a Magical Space with Rituals and Spells for the Home" - Arin Murphy-Hiscock

"The Magic of Herbs: Harnessing the Power of Nature" - Hecate Shaw

"The Magickal Year: Spells, Rituals, and Celebrations for Every Month." - D.J. Conway

"The Old Farmer's Almanac Gardening Calendar" - Old Farmer's Almanac

"The Secret Garden" - Frances Hodgson Burnett *(while fictional, it inspires ideas of gardening and nature)*

"The Secret of the Witch's Garden: 10 Simple Steps for Your Patch" - Sonya L. Melrose

"The Wild Garden: Expanded Edition" - William Robinson

"The Wild Wisdom of Weeds: 13 Essential Plants for Human Survival" - Katrina Blair

"The Woman's Book of Healing Herbs" - Kathi Keville

"Witchcraft and Herbcraft: The Joy of Earth and Nature" - T. H. Ryan

"Witchcraft and the Garden: Rituals and Recipes" - Nyssa Basarab

"Witchcraft in the Garden: An Everyday Approach" - M. Christine L. Jonestone

"Witch's Garden: The House of Light and Shadow" - Jason B. Dube

"Cottage Witchery: A Beginner's Guide" – Kimberly Renee

"Cottage Witch's Apothecary: A Practical Guide to Herbalism, Oils, Spells & Rituals" - Kimberly Renee

"Cottage Witch's Kitchen Witchery: Stirring Up Magick in the Kitchen" – Kimberly Renee

"Cottage Witch's: Guide to Self-Care Recipes, Spells & Rituals" – Kimberly Renee

"Kitchen Witchery for Everyday Magic: Bring Joy and

Positivity into Your Life with Restorative Rituals and Enchanting Recipes" – Regan Ralston

"The Book of Kitchen Witchery: Spells, recipes, and rituals for magical meals, an enchanted garden, and a happy home" – Cerridwen Greenleaf

"The Cottage Witch's Guide to Magic: 25 Enchanting Projects to Make Your Home More Sacred" – Suzzanne Lemmon

"The Encyclopedia of Kitchen Witchery" – Cassandra Sage

"The Green Witch: Your Complete Guide to the Natural Magic of Herbs, Flowers, Essential Oils, and More" – Arin Murphy-Hiscock

"The Green Witch's Grimoire: Your Complete Guide to Creating Your Own Book of Natural Magic" – Arin Murphy-Hiscock

"The Kitchen Witch Handbook: Wisdom, Recipes, and Potions for Everyday Magic at Home" – Aurora Kane

# Personal Thank You

I wanted to take a moment to extend my heartfelt thanks to each and every one of you who has purchased and read my book, *Cottage Witchery: Book of Shadows & Practical Magick*. Your support and enthusiasm mean the world to me.

Writing this book was a labor of love, born from my passion for the art and practice of cottage witchery. Knowing that my words have found a place in your homes and hearts is truly humbling. I hope the insights, spells, and rituals within its pages have inspired you and helped you connect more deeply with your own magickal practice.

I am grateful for the stories and experiences you've shared with me, as they remind me of the beauty of community and the shared journey we are on. Your encouragement keeps my creative spirit alive, and I look forward to continuing this adventure with all of you.

Thank you once again for your support. May your paths be illuminated with love, light, and enchanting magick.

With all my gratitude,

*Kimberly Renee*

# About The Author

## Kimberly Renee

Kimberly Renee is the author of many books, both fiction and non-fiction, including subjects of business, spirituality, and wellness subjects. When she is not writing, she spends her time with her husband and her fur baby in the eastern U.S.A.

Made in United States
Orlando, FL
10 December 2024